GRATEFUL DEAD

WORKINGMAN'S DEAD

Transcribed by Hemme Luttjeboer and Danny Begelman

Copyright © MMV by Alfred Publishing Co., Inc.
All rights reserved. Printed in USA.

ISBN 0-7579-4163-9 (Book)

GRATEFUL DEAD

WORKINGMAN'S DEAD

CONTENTS

UNCLE JOHN'S BAND	3
HIGH TIME	12
DIRE WOLF	17
NEW SPEEDWAY BOOGIE	30
CUMBERLAND BLUES	48
BLACK PETER	72
EASY WIND	91
CASEY JONES	102

UNCLE JOHN'S BAND

Words by ROBERT HUNTER
Music by JERRY GARCIA

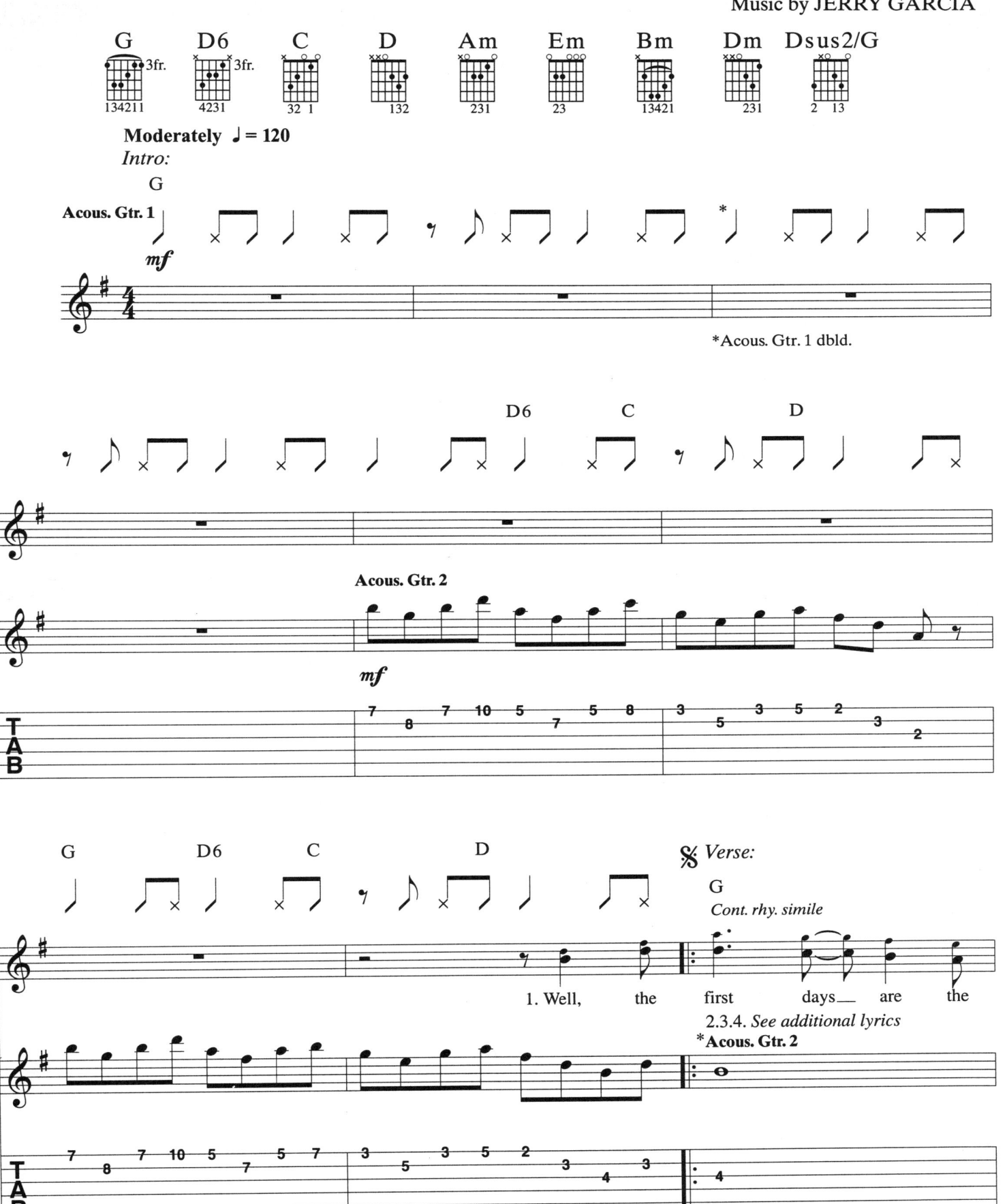

Chords: G   D6   C   D   Am   Em   Bm   Dm   Dsus2/G

Moderately ♩ = 120

Intro:

Acous. Gtr. 1

Acous. Gtr. 1 dbld.

Acous. Gtr. 2

Verse:
Cont. rhy. simile

1. Well, the first days are the
2. 3. 4. See additional lyrics

Acous. Gtr. 2

Acous. Gtr. 2 simile on repeats.

Uncle John's Band - 9 - 1

© 1970 (Renewed) ICE NINE PUBLISHING CO., INC.
All Rights Reserved

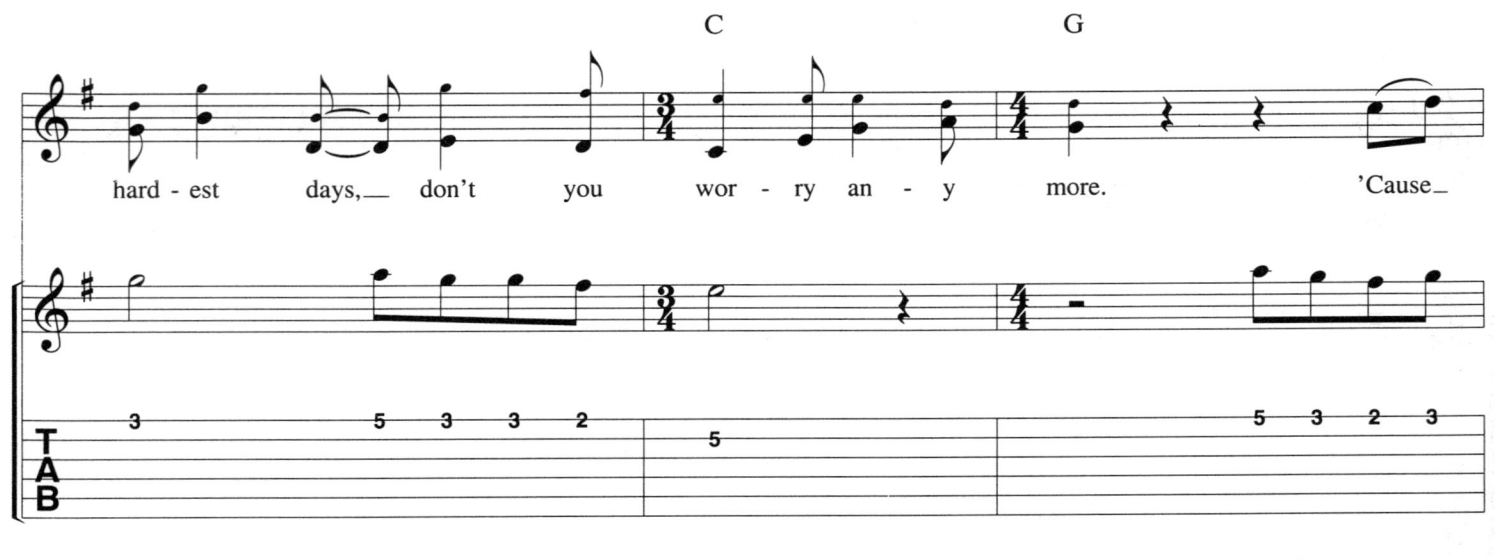

Uncle John's Band - 9 - 2

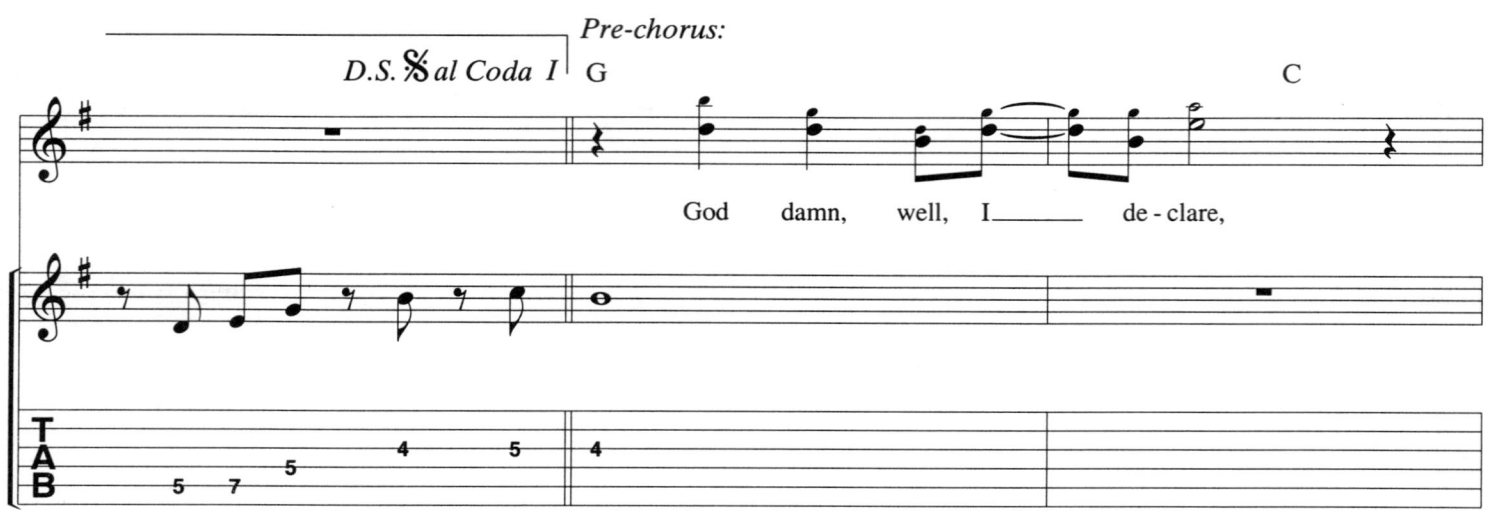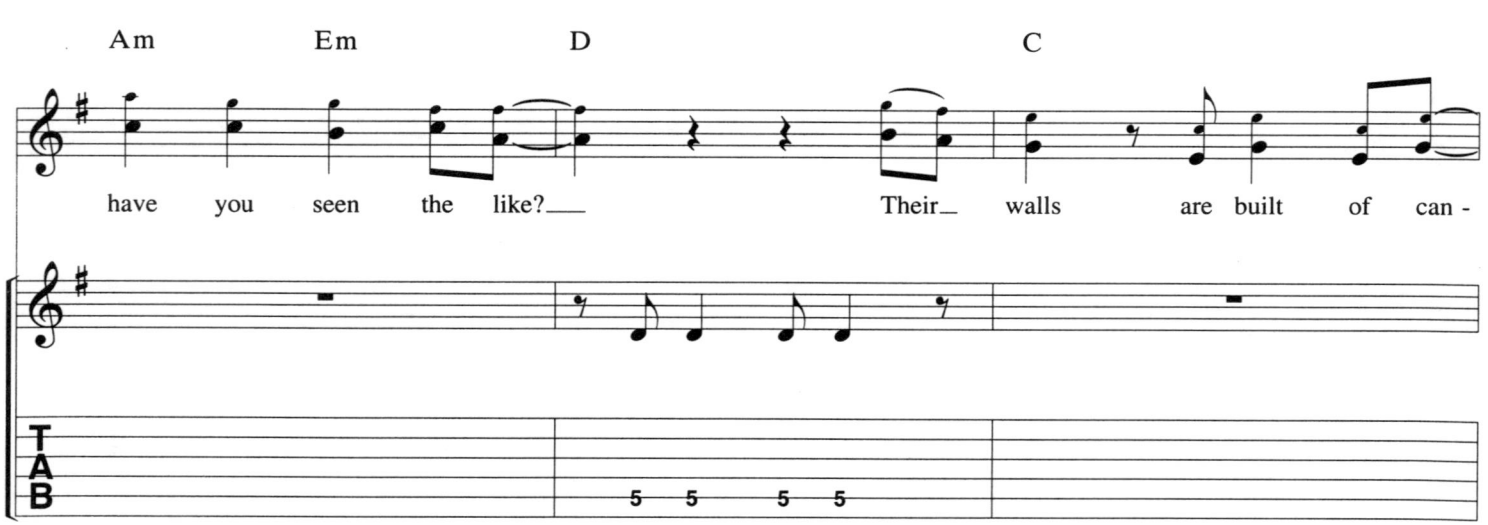

Chorus:

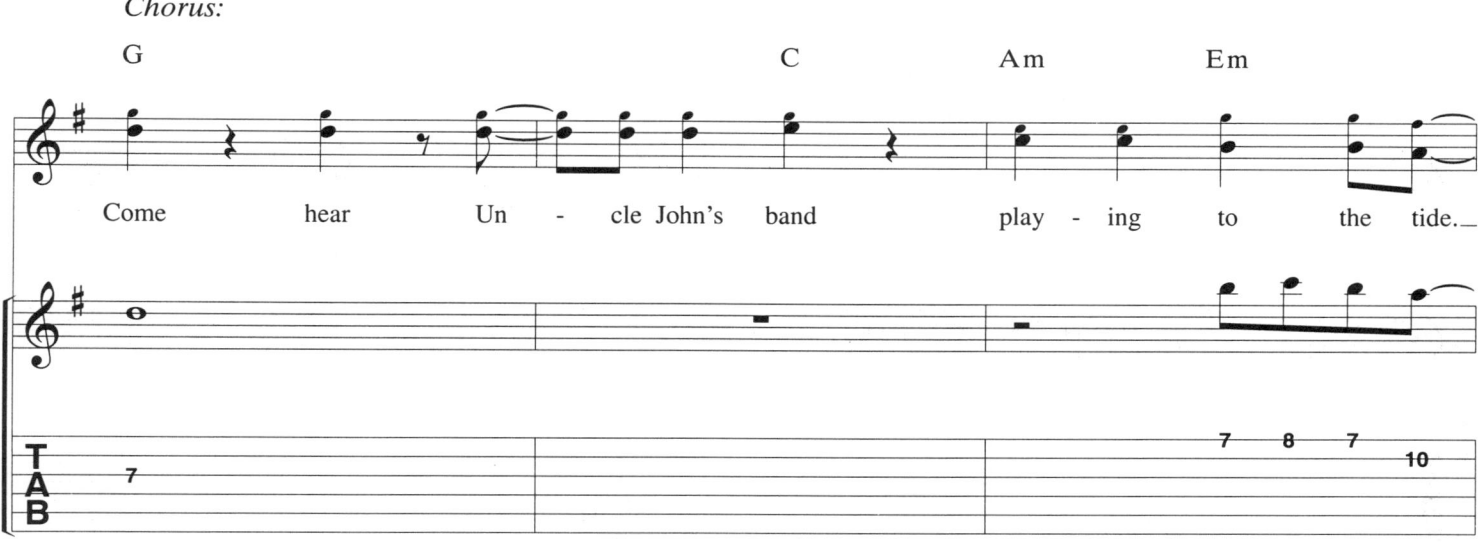

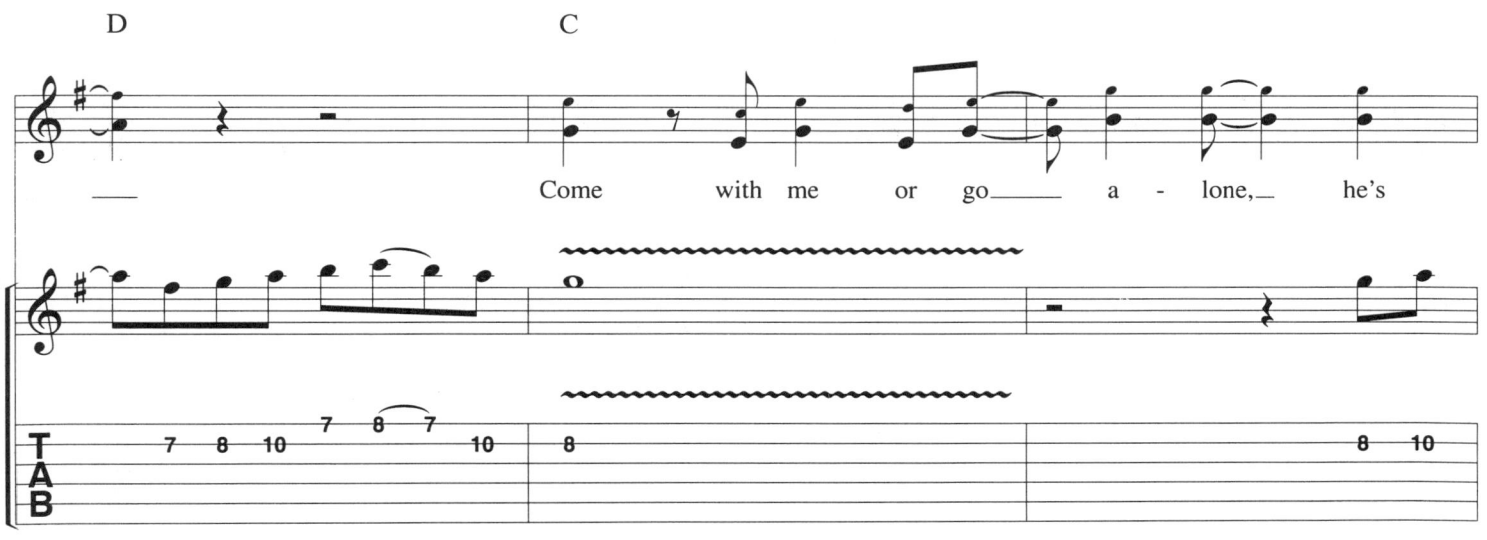

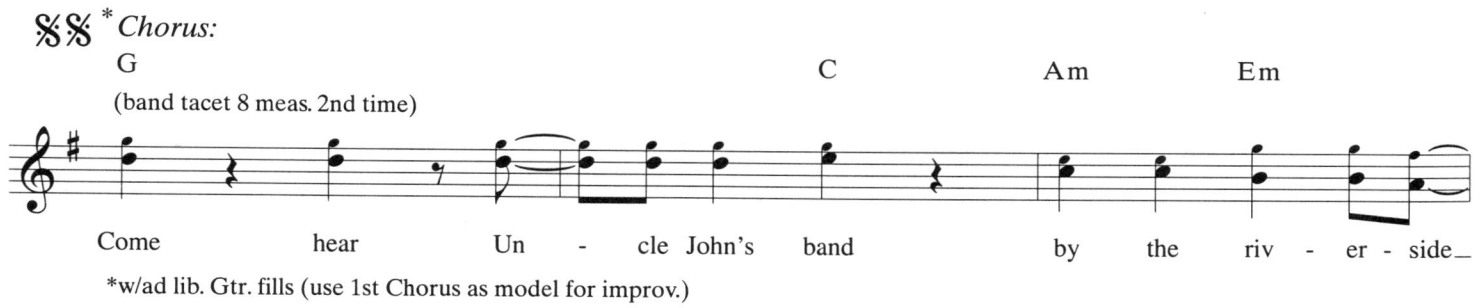

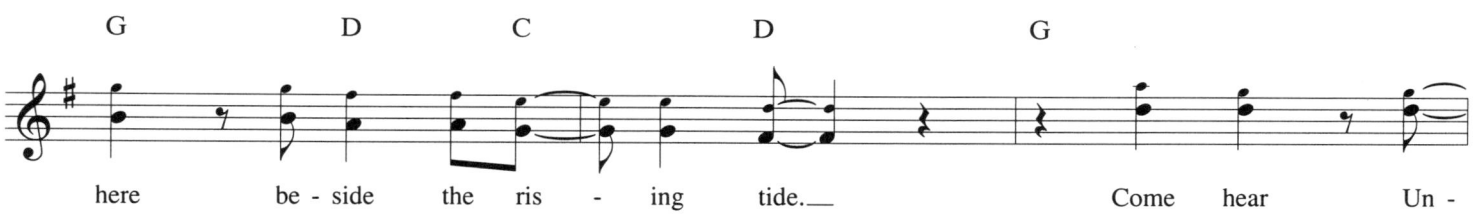
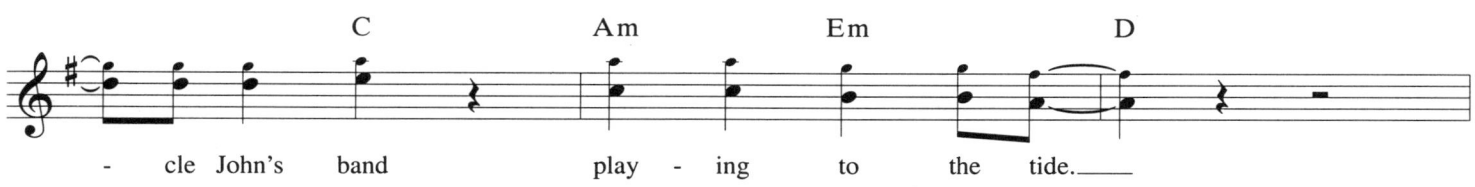
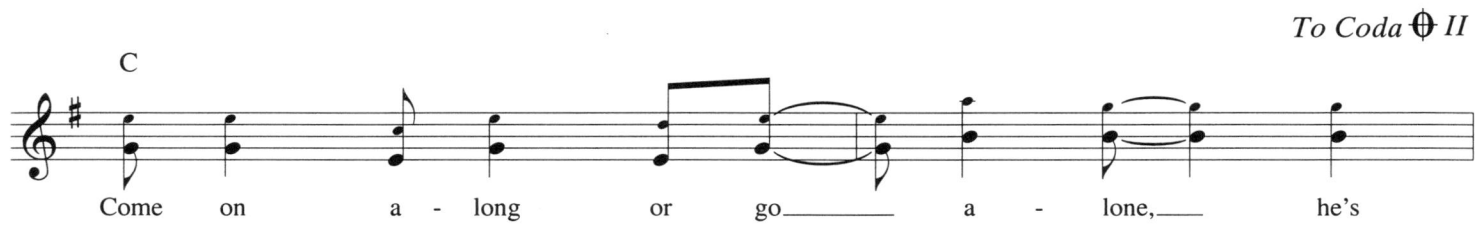
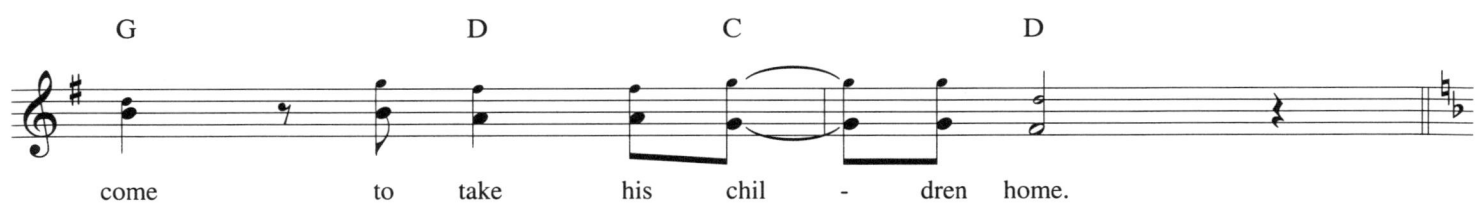

Interlude 2:
Dm
G
C
Play 7 times
Dm
Acous. Gtr. 2
hold
TAB
Wo - oh, what I want to know...
(hold)
TAB
C
G
N.C.
D.S. 𝄋𝄋 al Coda II
how does the song go?
TAB

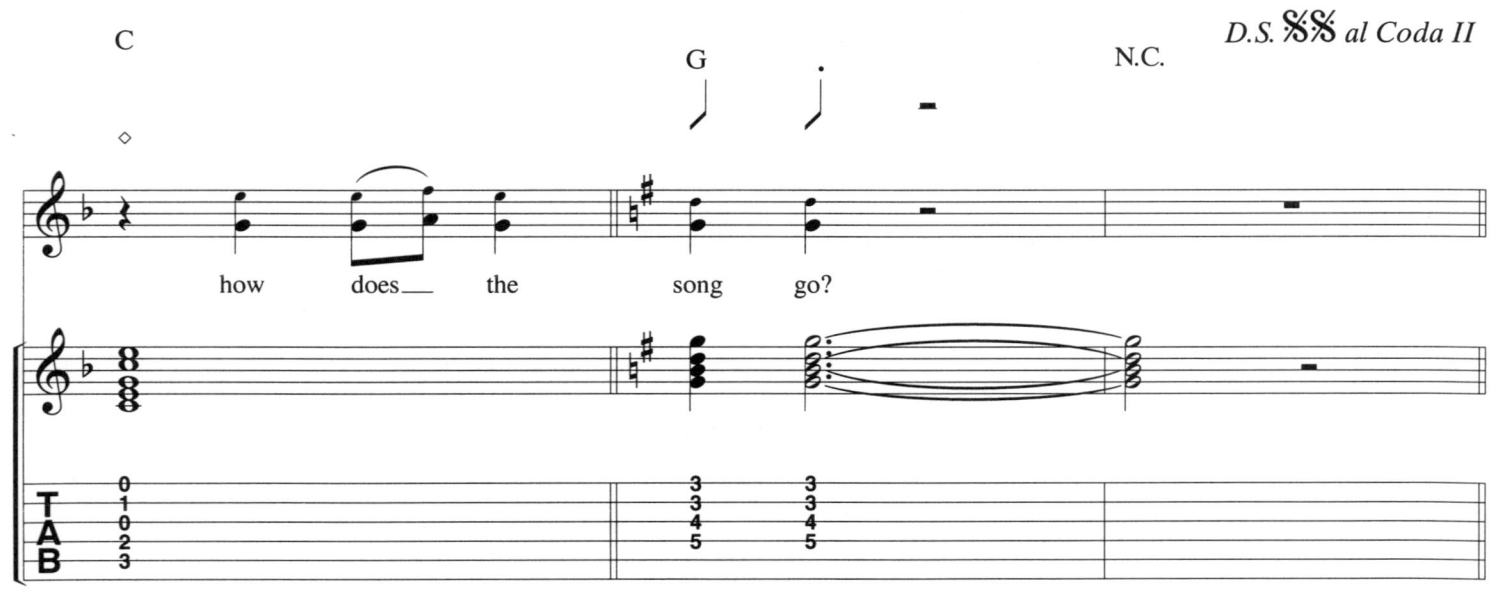

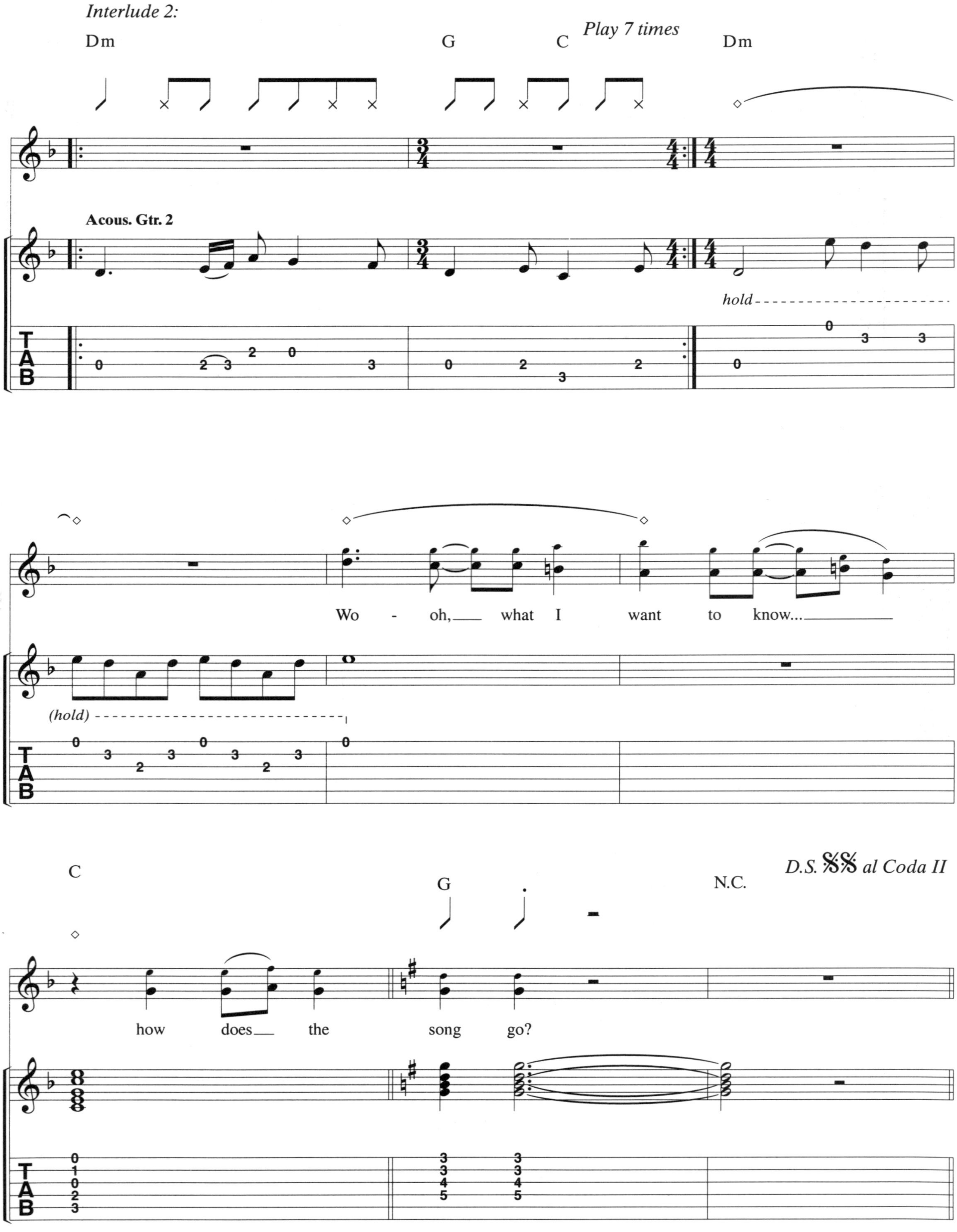

Verse 2:
It's a buck dancer's choice, my friend, better take my advice.
You know all the rules by now and the fire from the ice.
Will you come with me?
Won't you come with me?
Wo-oh, what I want to know; will you come with me?
(To Pre-chorus:)

Verse 3:
It's the same story the crow told me, it's the only one he knows.
Like the morning sun you come and like the wind you go.
Ain't no time to hate, barely time to wait.
Wo-oh, what I want to know; where does the time go?
(To Verse 4:)

Verse 4:
I live in a silver mine and I call it Beggar's Tomb.
I got me a violin and I beg you call the tune.
Anybody's choice, I can hear your voice.
Wo-oh, what I want to know; how does the song go?
(To Chorus:)

High Time - 5 - 3

Verse 2:
The wheels are muddy, got a ton of hay.
Now listen here, baby, 'cause I mean what I say.
I'm having a high time, living the good life, ah, well, I know.
(To Bridge:)

Verse 3:
Tomorrow come trouble, tomorrow come pain.
Now don't think too hard, baby, 'cause you know what I'm saying.
I could show you a high time, living the good life, ah, don't be that way.

Verse 4:
Nothing's for certain, it could always go wrong.
Come in when it's raining, go on out when it's gone.
We could have us a high time, living the good life, ah, well, I know.

DIRE WOLF

Words by ROBERT HUNTER
Music by JERRY GARCIA

*Pedal steel gtr. arranged for electric gtr.

Dire Wolf - 13 - 1

© 1970 (Renewed) ICE NINE PUBLISHING CO., INC.
All Rights Reserved

Dire Wolf - 13 - 2

Dire Wolf - 13 - 4

E
hold
hold
hold
hold
D
E
A
C♯7
F♯m
E
Oo,
oo,
oo.
hold bend
hold
hold
8va

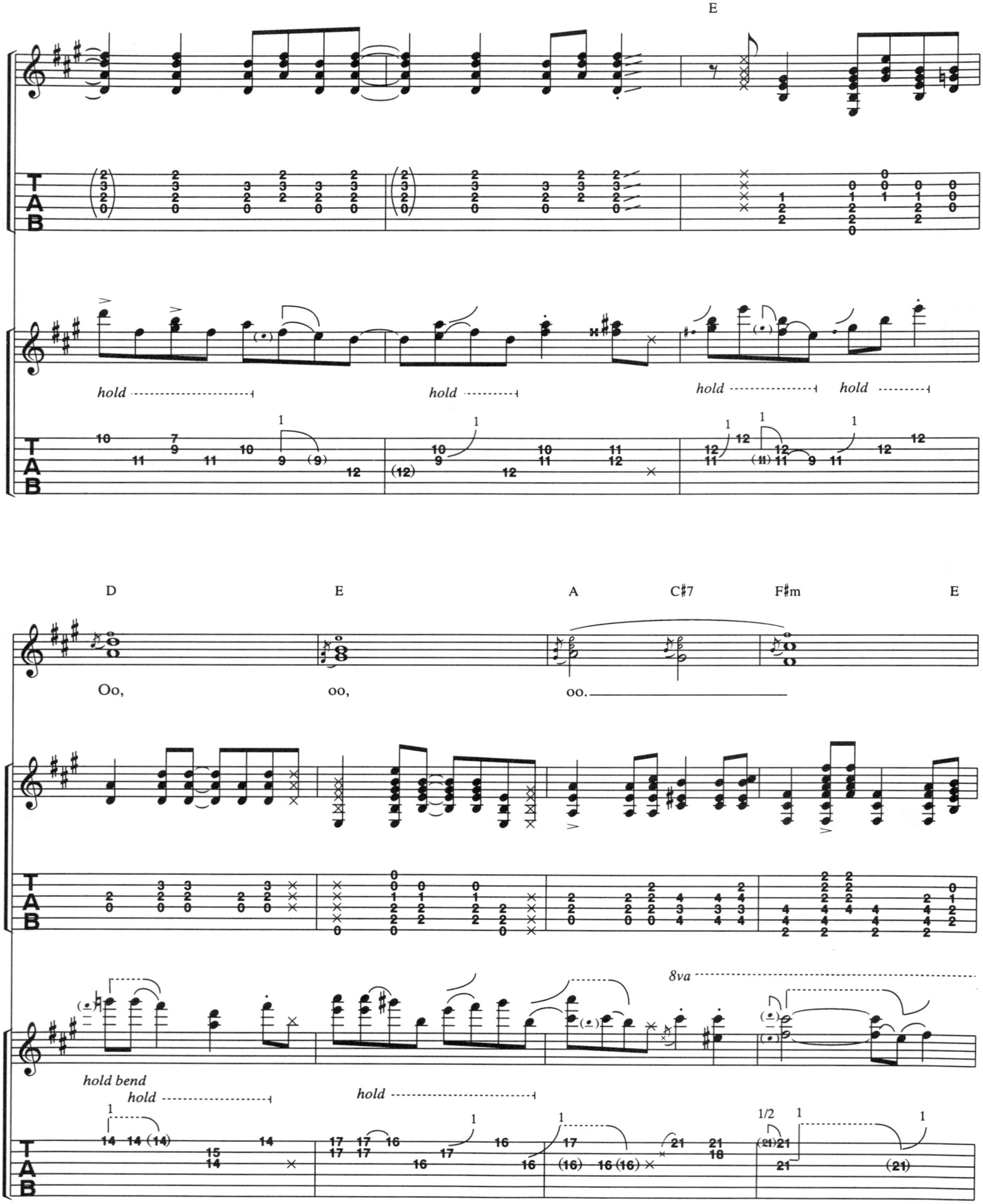

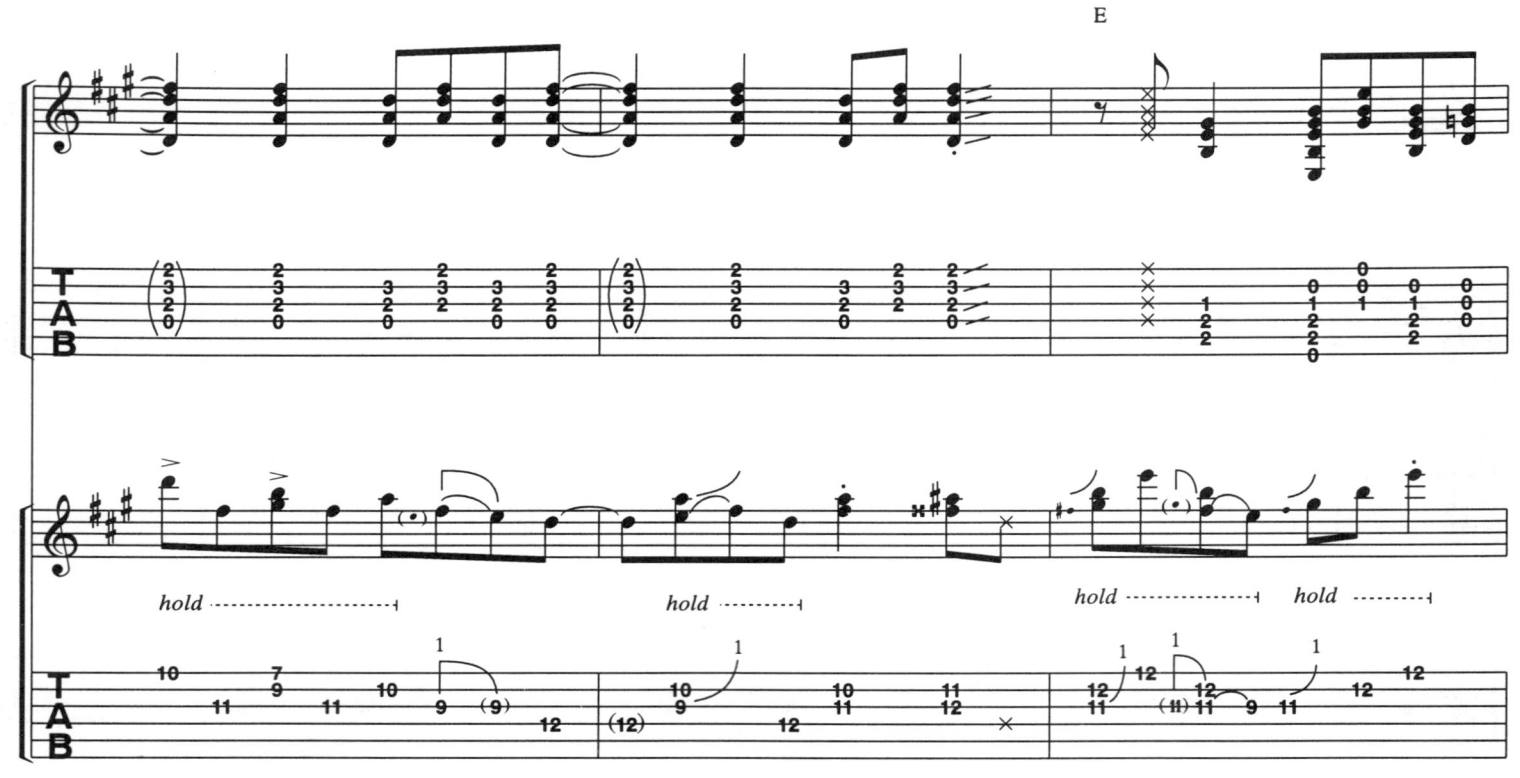

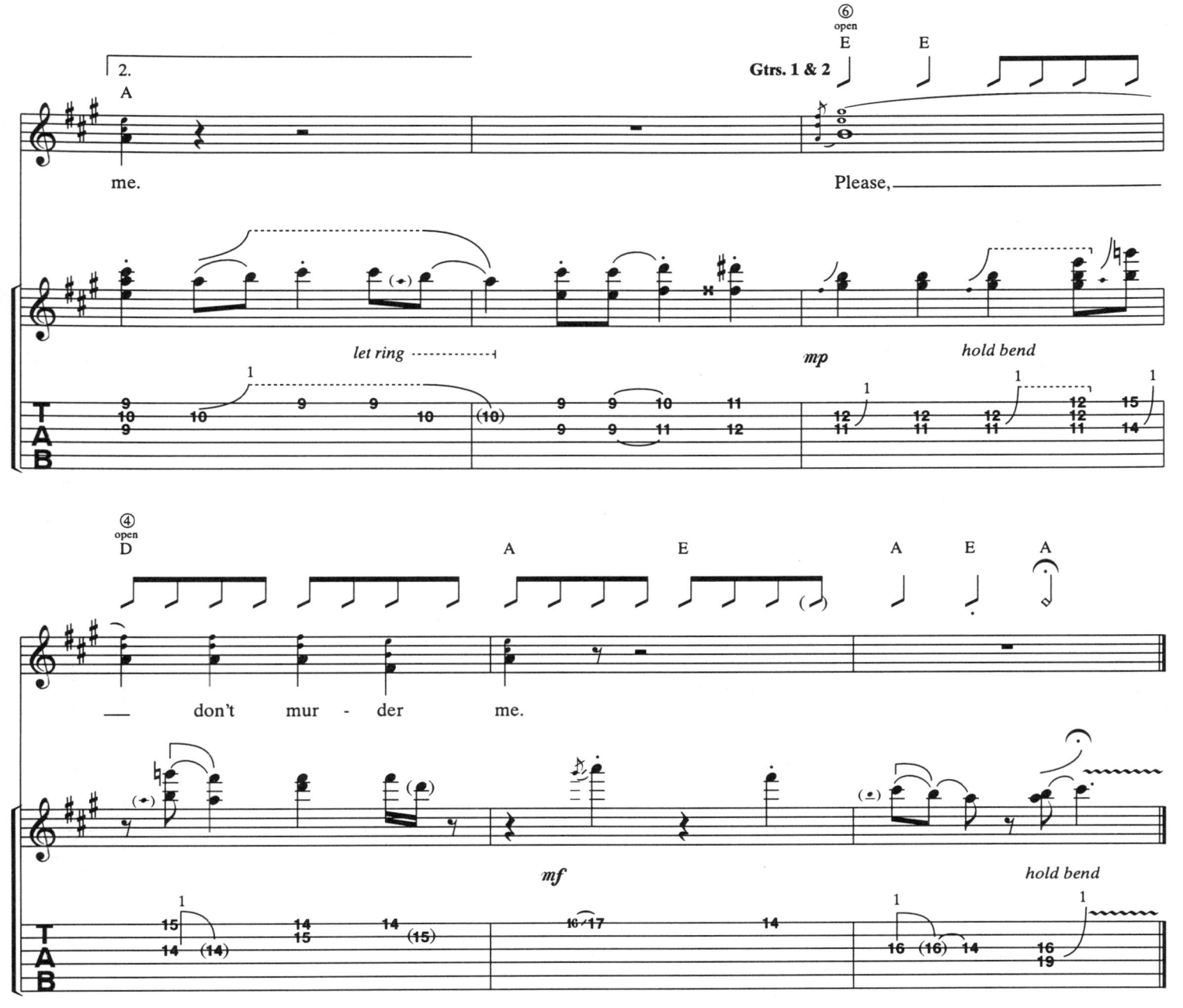

Verse 4:
The wolf came in, I got my cards,
We sat down for a game.
I cut my deck to the queen of hearts
But the cards were all the same;
Don't murder me...
(To Chorus:)

Verse 5:
In the back-wash of Fennario,
The black and bloody mire,
The dire wolf collects his due
While the boys sing around the fire:
Don't murder me...
(To Chorus:)

NEW SPEEDWAY BOOGIE

Words by ROBERT HUNTER
Music by JERRY GARCIA

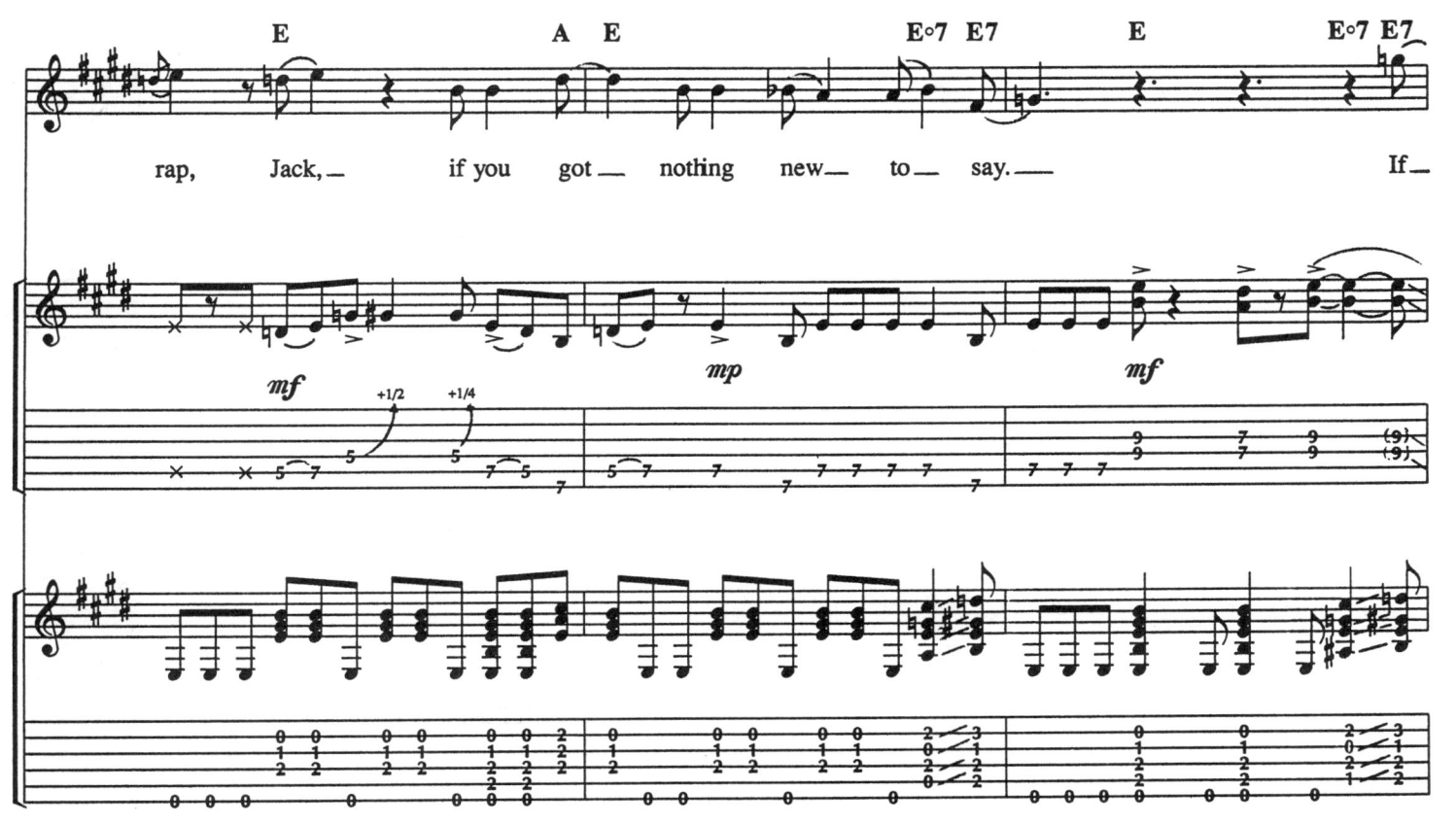

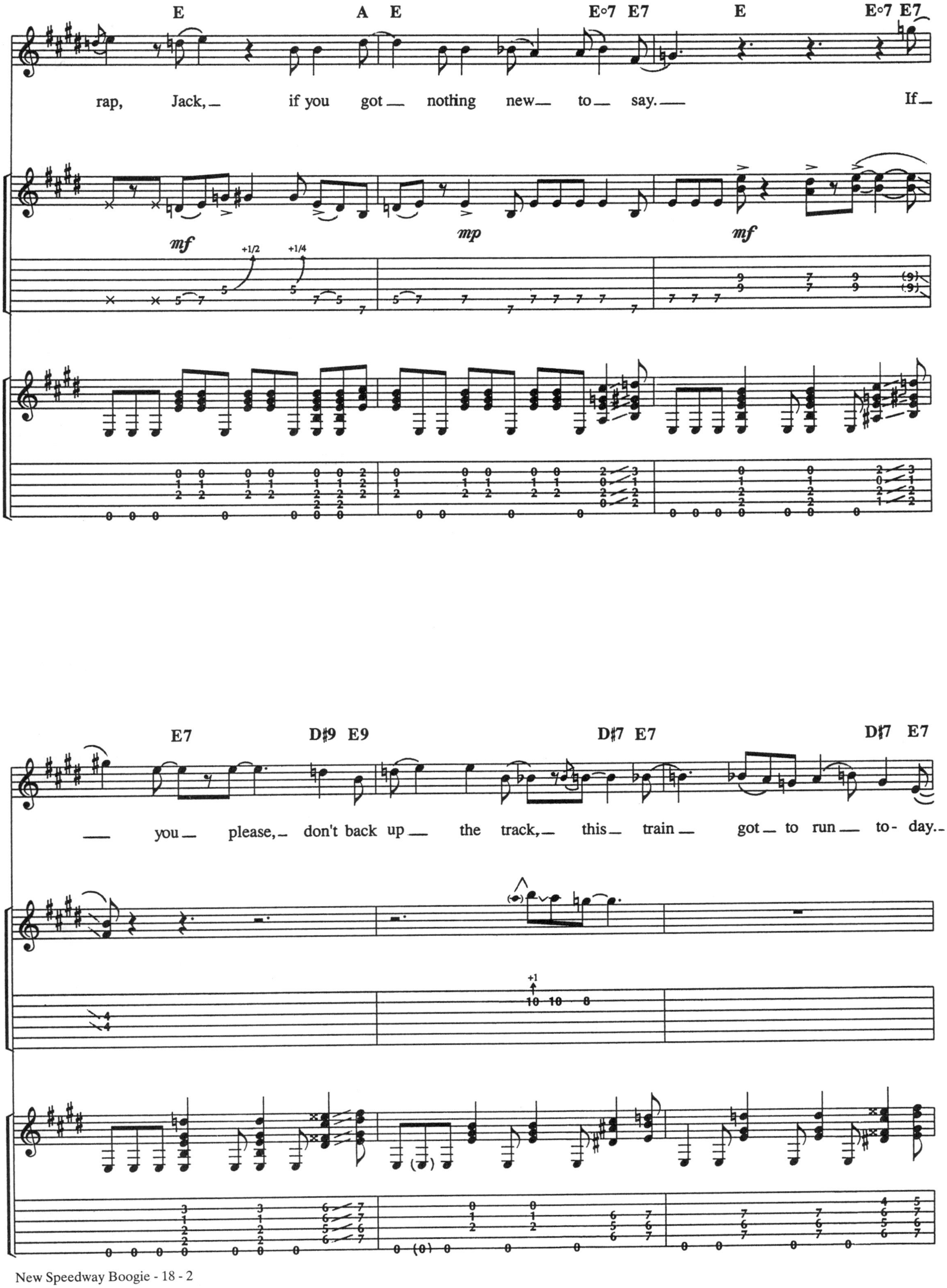
E A E E°7 E7 E E°7 E7
rap, Jack, if you got nothing new to say. If
mf
mp
mf
+1/2
+1/4
E7 D♯9 E9 D♯7 E7 D♯7 E7
you please, don't back up the track, this train got to run to- day.
+1

I spend a lit-tle time on the moun-tain,

spent a lit-tle time on the hill. (on the hill) I heard some say "Bet-ter run a-way," others say "Bet-ter stand still." Now

I don't know but I've been told it's hard to run with the

A Asus4 A E°7 E7 E°7 E7
weight_ of gold._ The oth - er_ hand_ I had heard it_ said,_ it's just_
mp
G D A Asus2 A Asus2 A5 A E°7
_ as hard_ with a weight_ of lead._
p
Steady gliss.

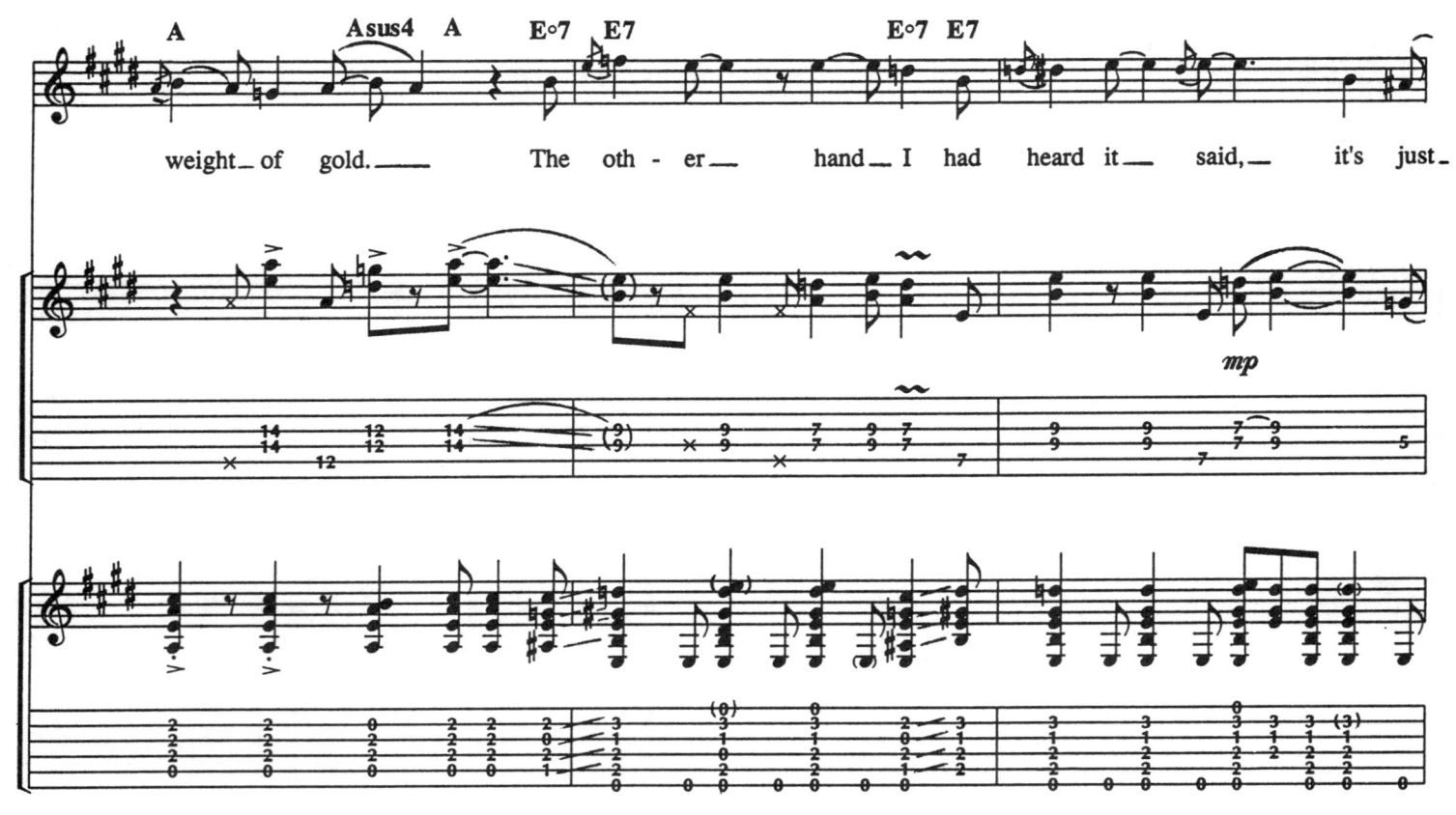

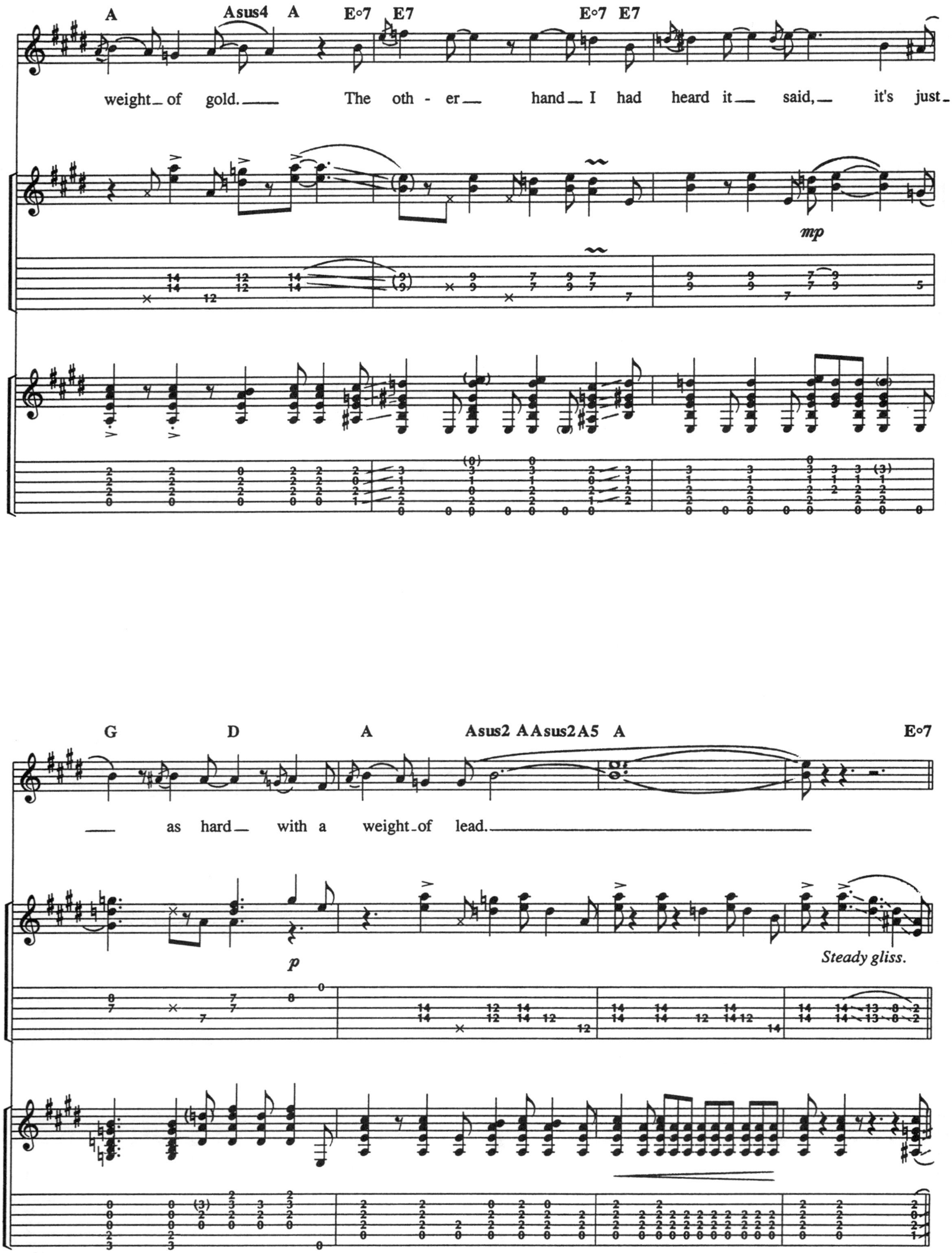

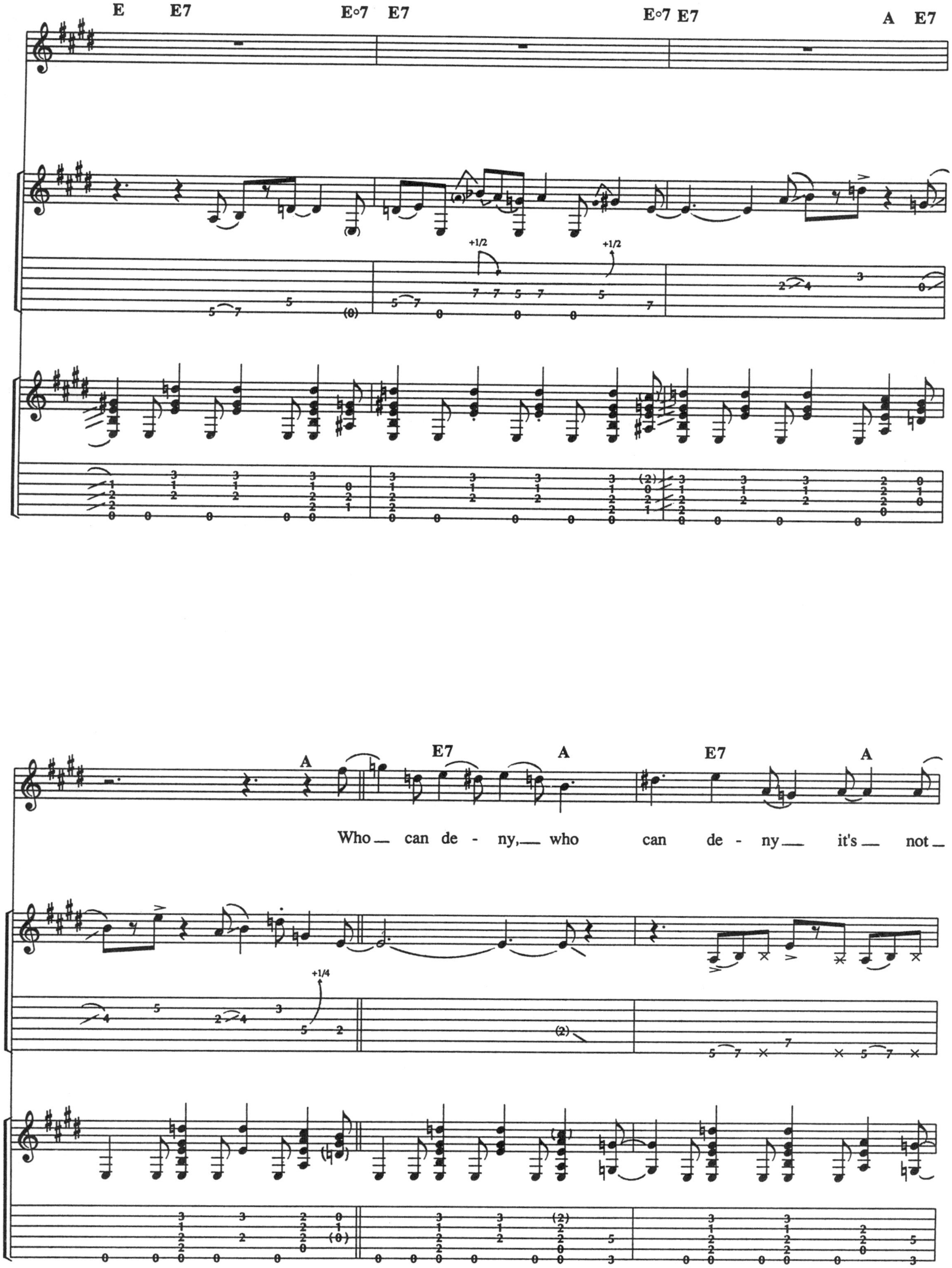
E
E7
E°7
E7
E°7
E7
A
E7
A
E7
A
E7
A
Who can de - ny, who can de - ny it's not

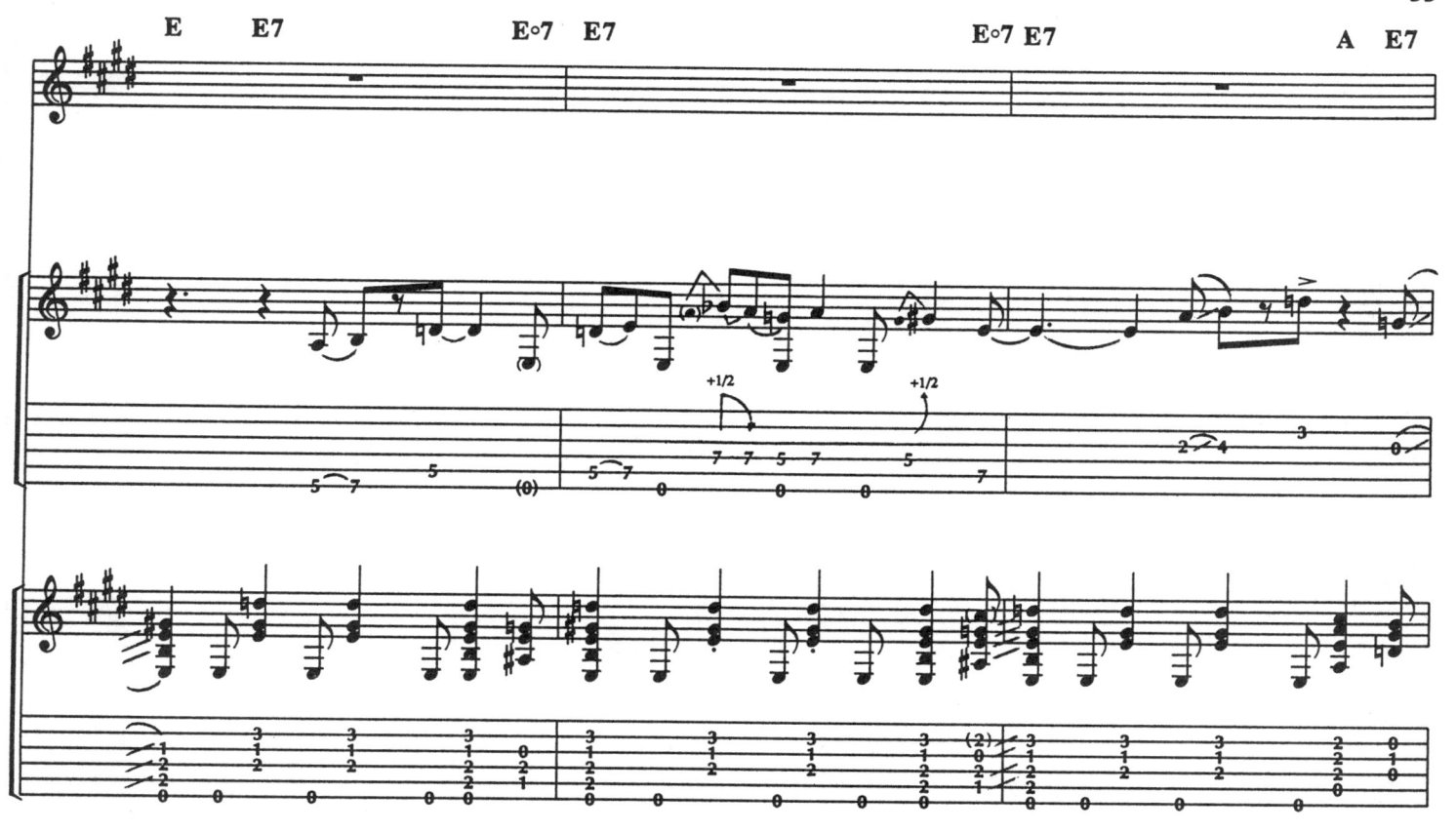

36

New Speedway Boogie - 18 - 7

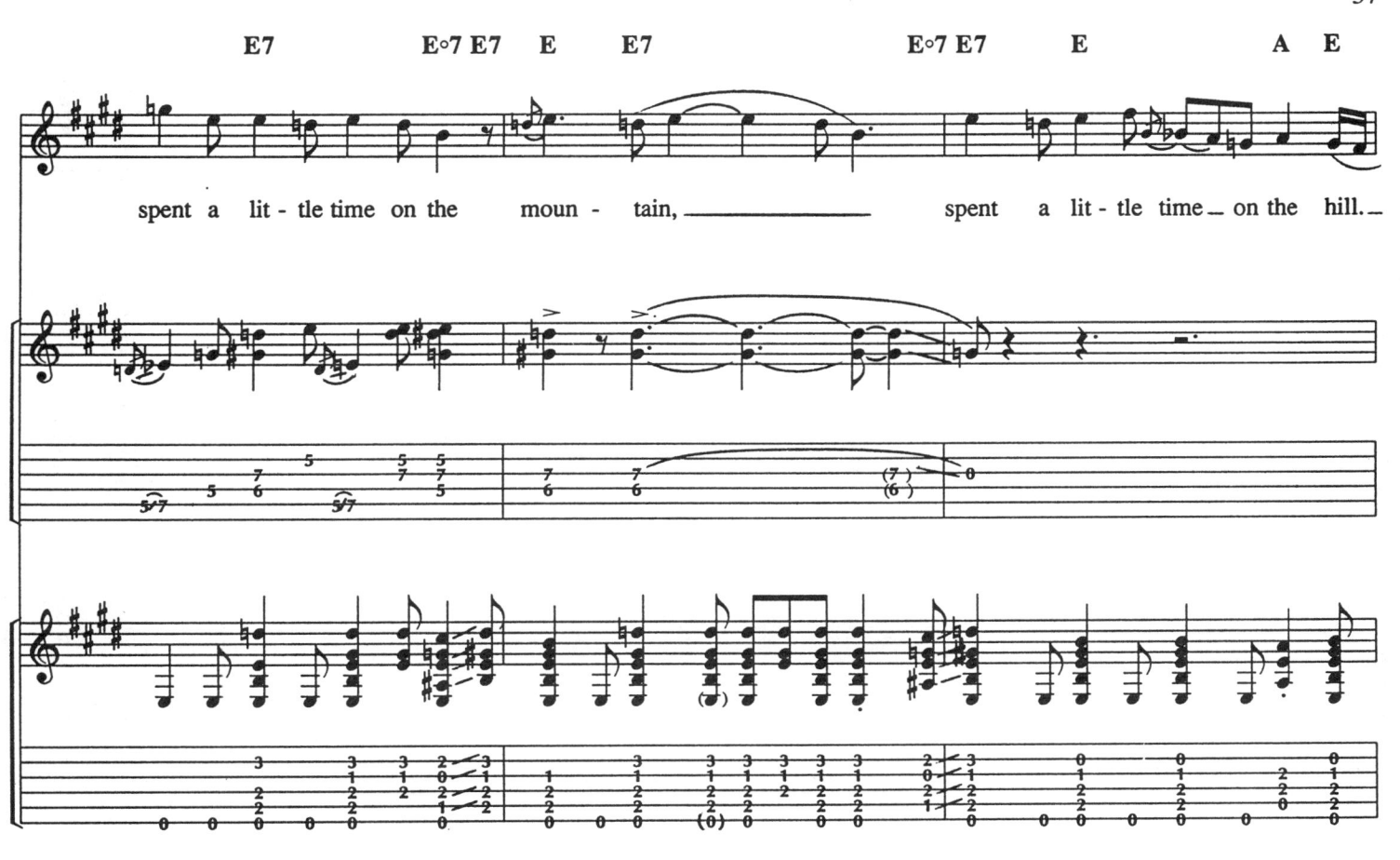

spent a lit-tle time on the moun-tain, _____ spent a lit-tle time ___ on the hill. ___

___ (on the hill) ___ Things ___ went down ___ we don't ___ un-der-stand ___ but I think ___

G D A G E A E
— in — time — we will. — Now I — don't — know — but
A E G D A Asus2 A G
I was — told — in the heat of the sun — a man — died — of cold. —
p mf

Keep on _____ com-ing or ____ stand __ and wait, __ with the sun ___ so dark and the

(Hour so late) _____

hour so late. _____

Steady gliss.

New Speedway Boogie - 18 - 10

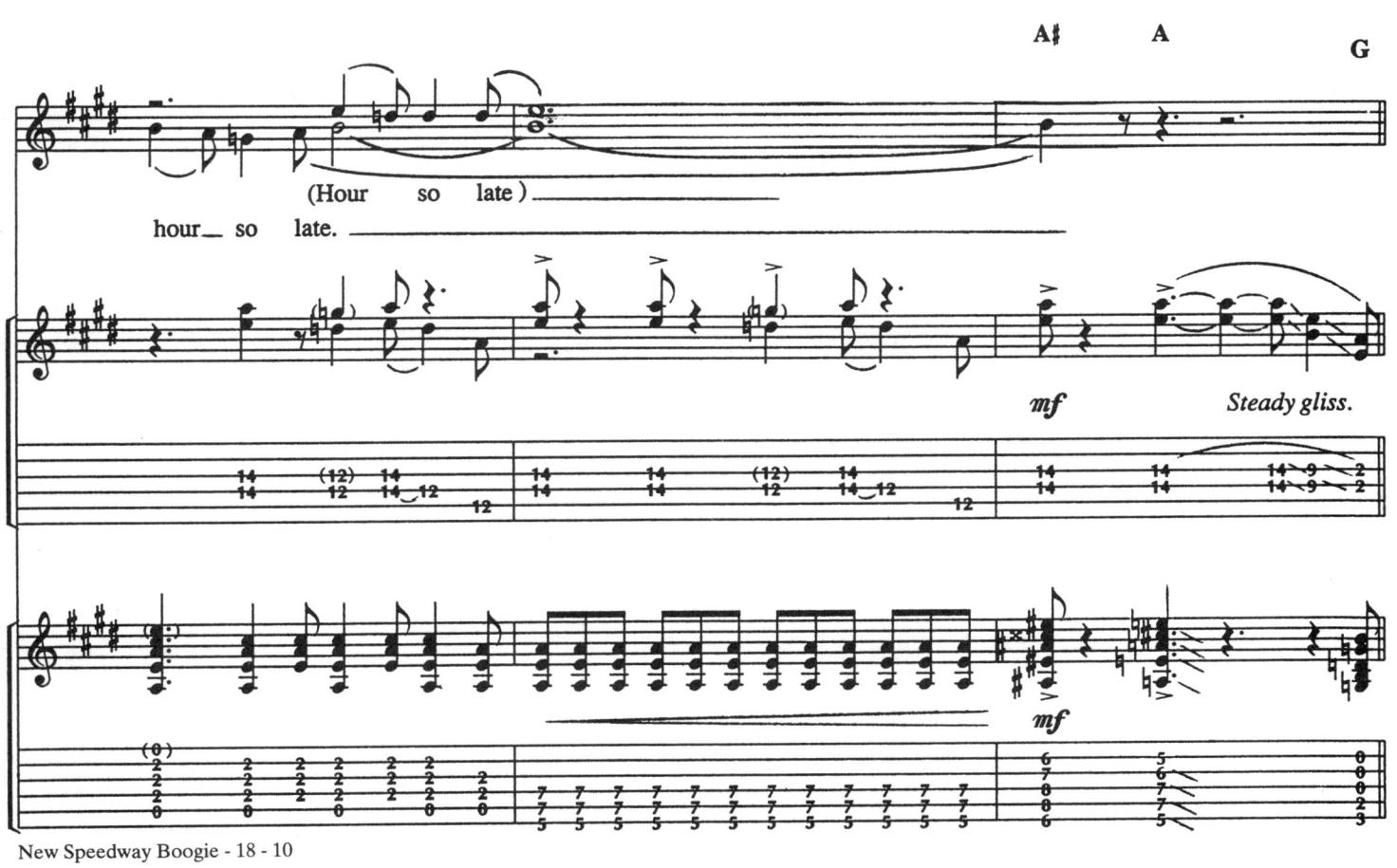

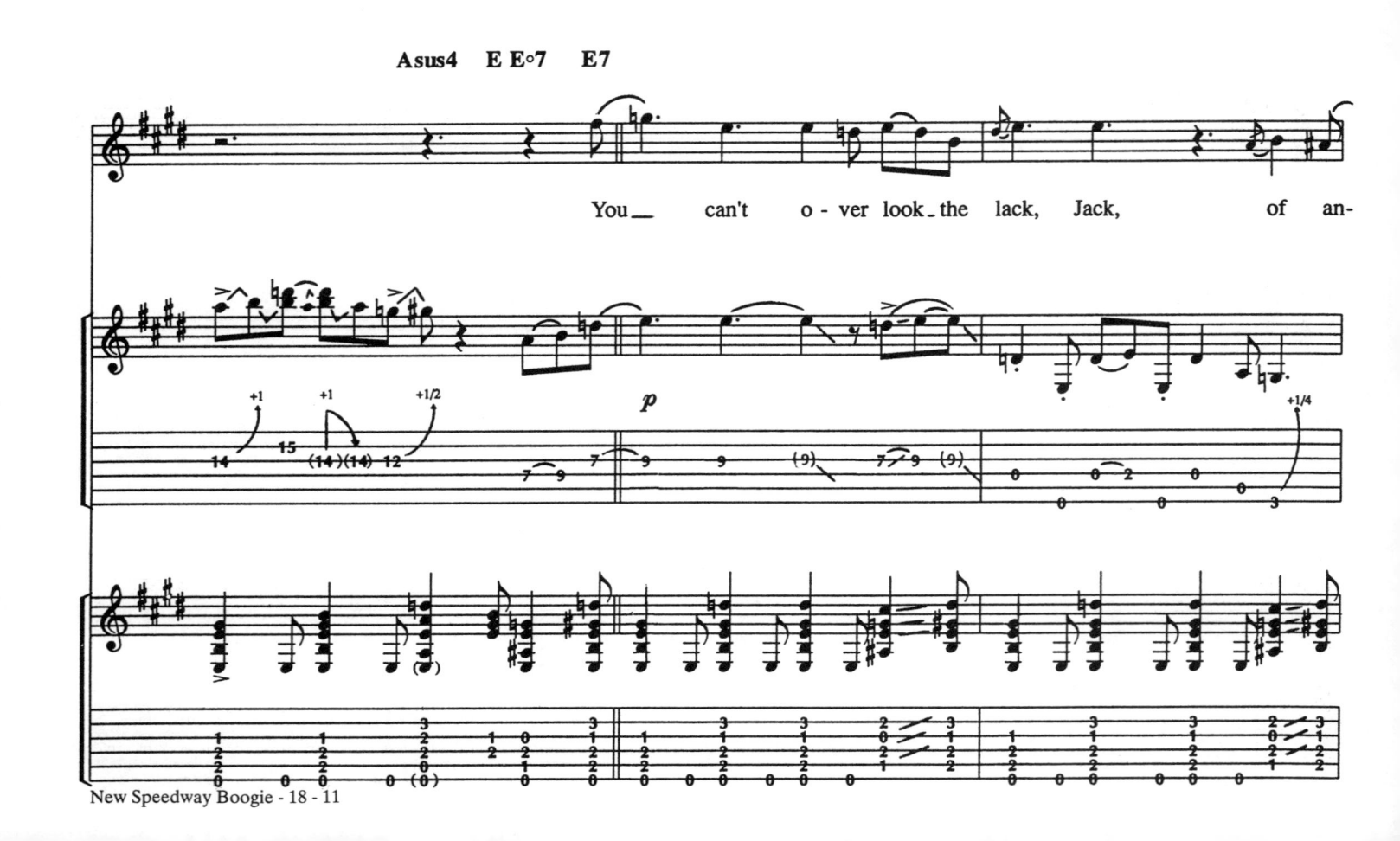

You can't o-ver look the lack, Jack, of an-

y other highway to ride. It's got no signs or dividing lines, and very few rules to guide. I spent a lit-tle time on the moun-tain, _____ spent a lit-tle time on the hill._

(on the hill.)____ Well, I saw_ things_ get-ting out of hand,__ I guess

43

they always will. Now, I don't know, but

I've been told, if the horse don't pull you got to carry the load

New Speedway Boogie - 18 - 14

44

I don't know who's back's that strong; may-be find out be-fore too long.

Steady gliss.

New Speedway Boogie - 18 - 15

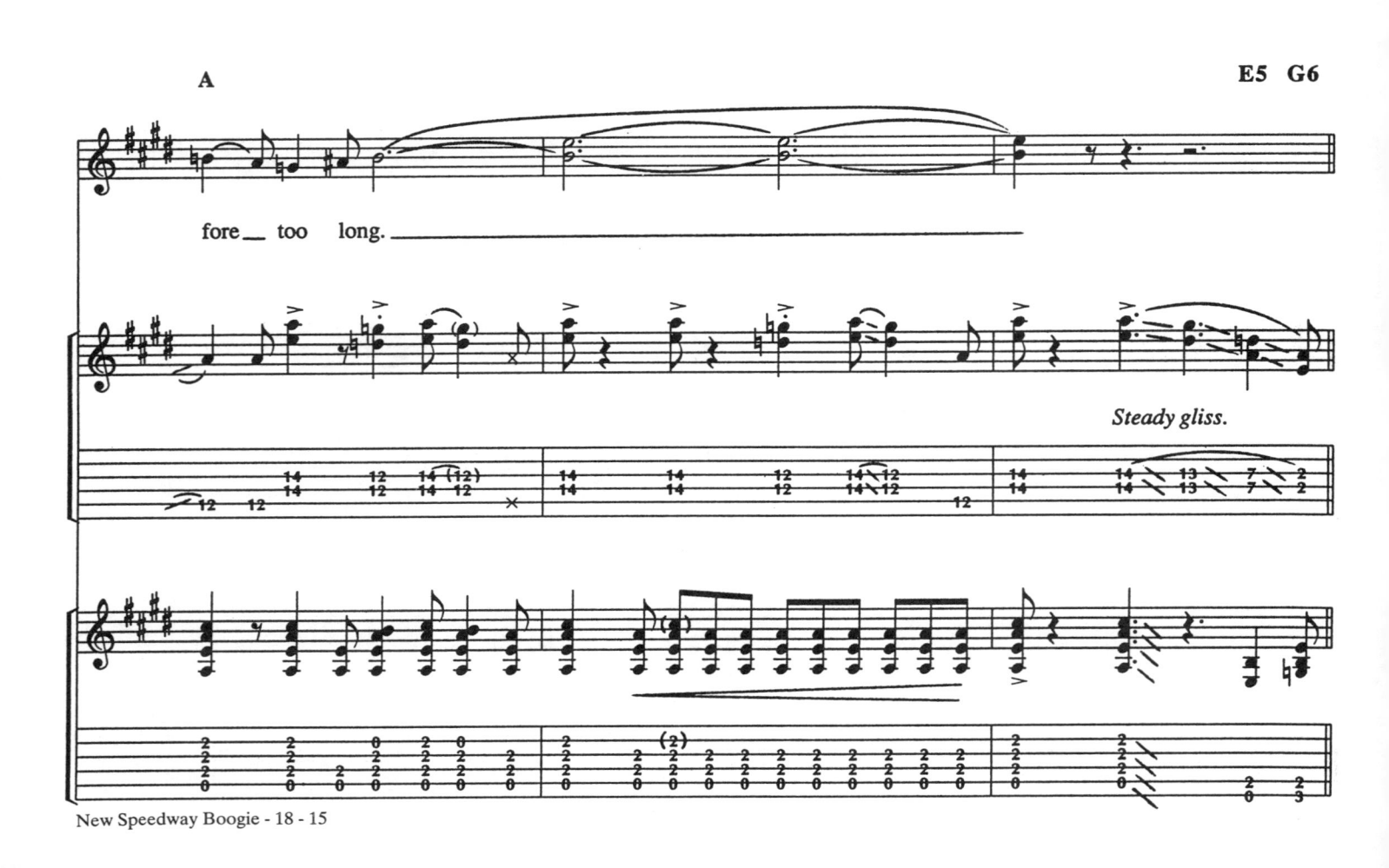

45

Play 3 times

One way or an-oth-er,___ One way or an-oth-er,___ One way or an-oth-er,___ this dark-

New Speedway Boogie - 18 - 16

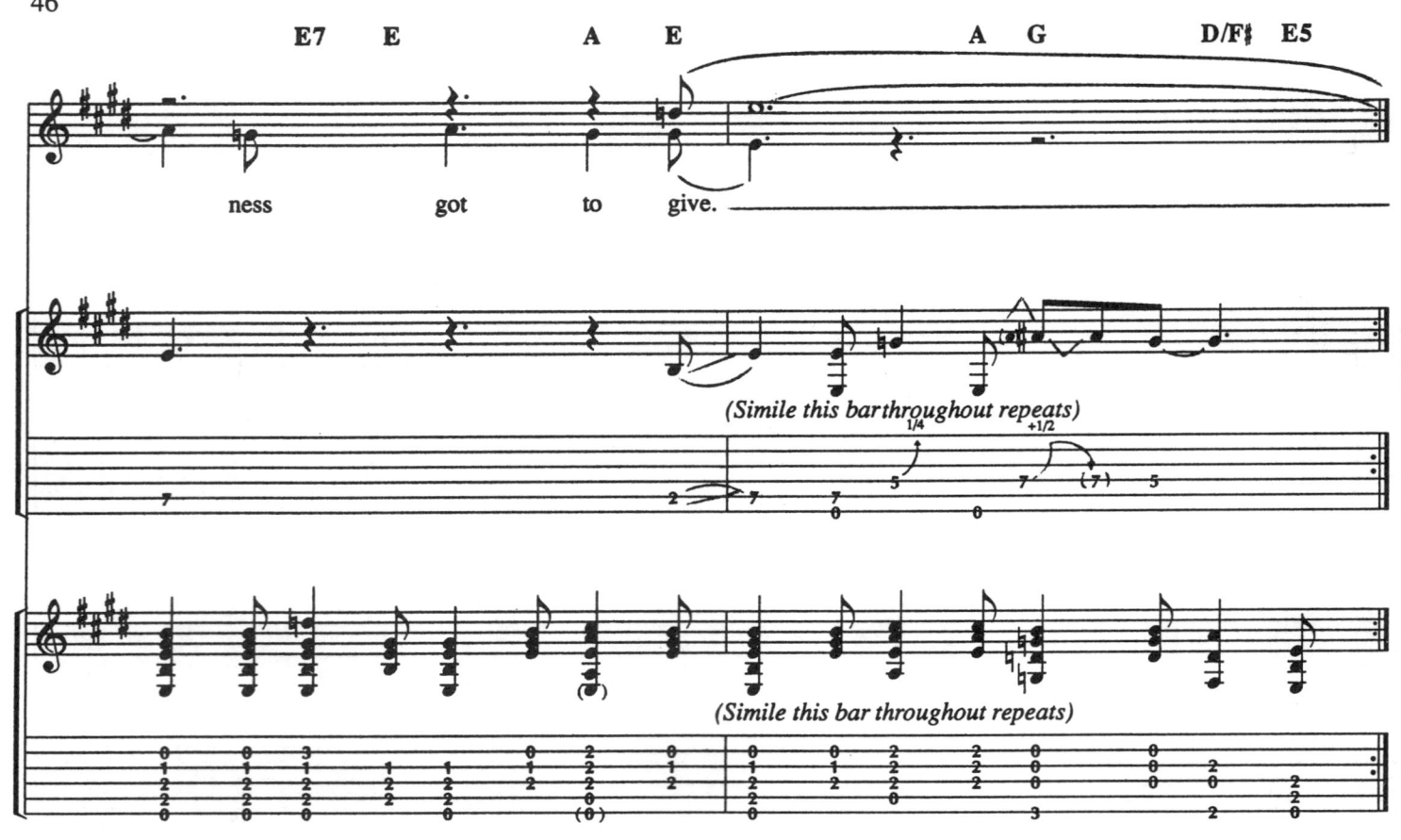

ness got to give.

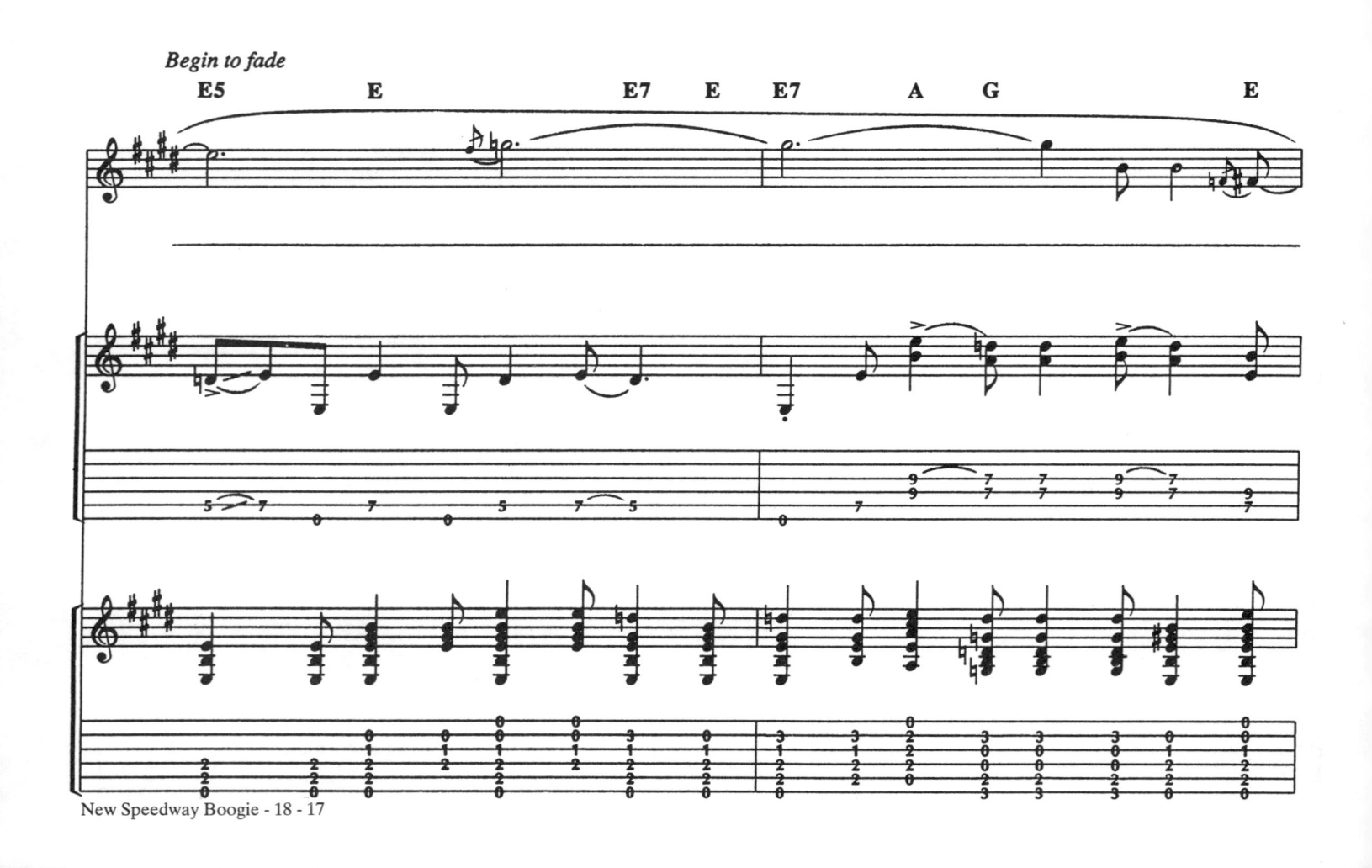

(Simile this bar throughout repeats)

(Simile this bar throughout repeats)

Begin to fade

Oo!

Fade out

New Speedway Boogie - 18 - 18

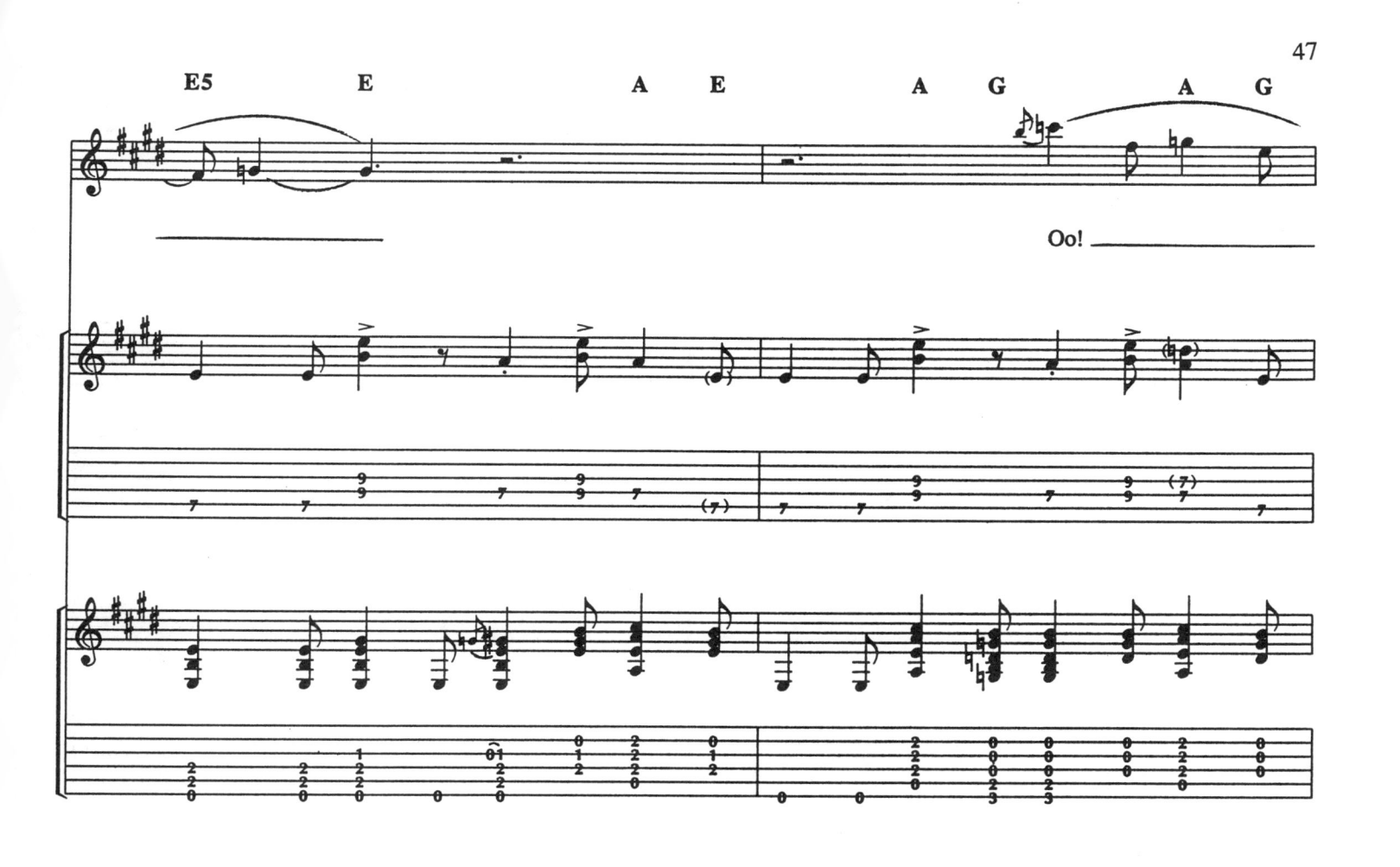

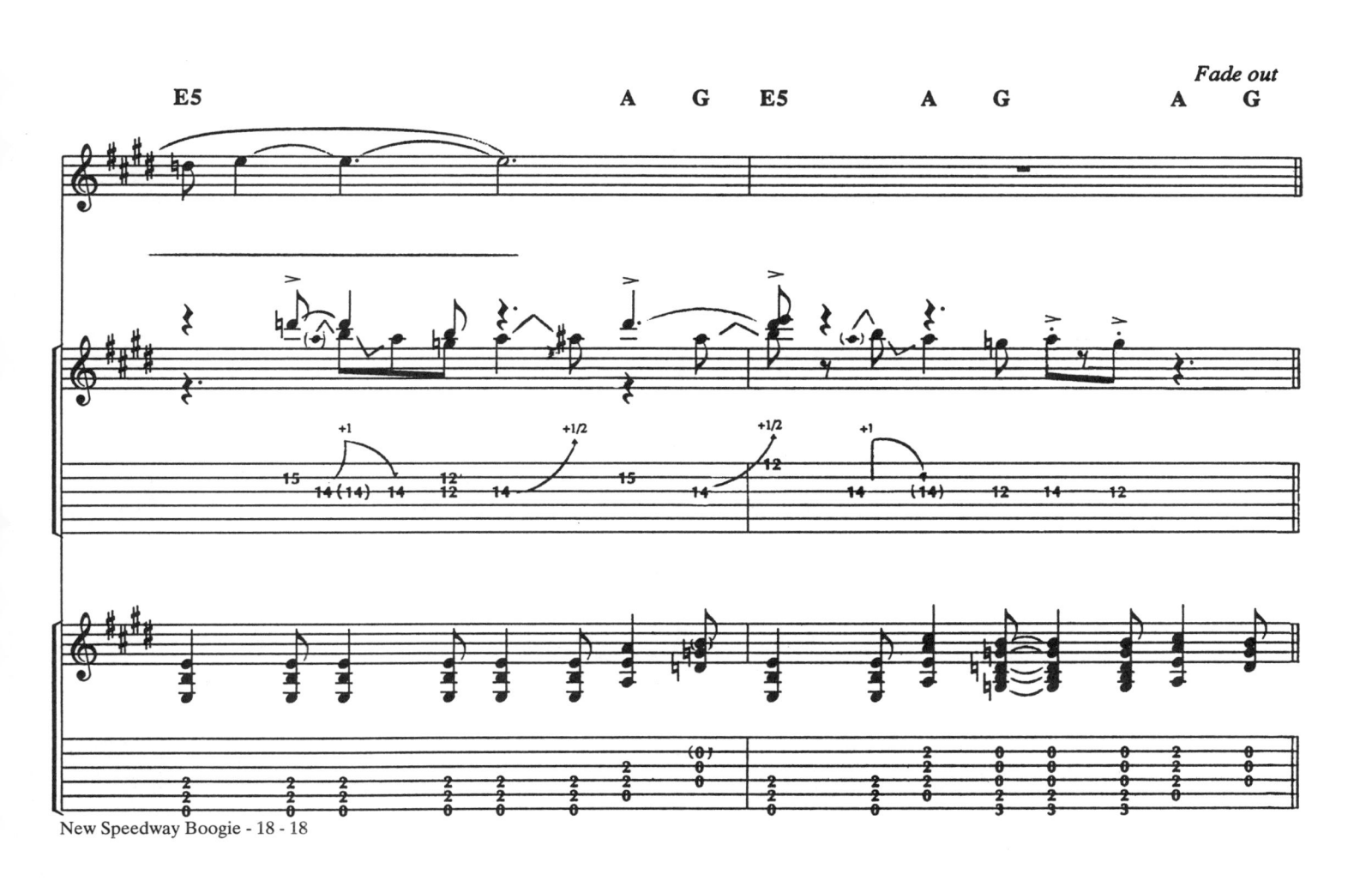

CUMBERLAND BLUES

Words by ROBERT HUNTER
Music by JERRY GARCIA and PHILIP LESH

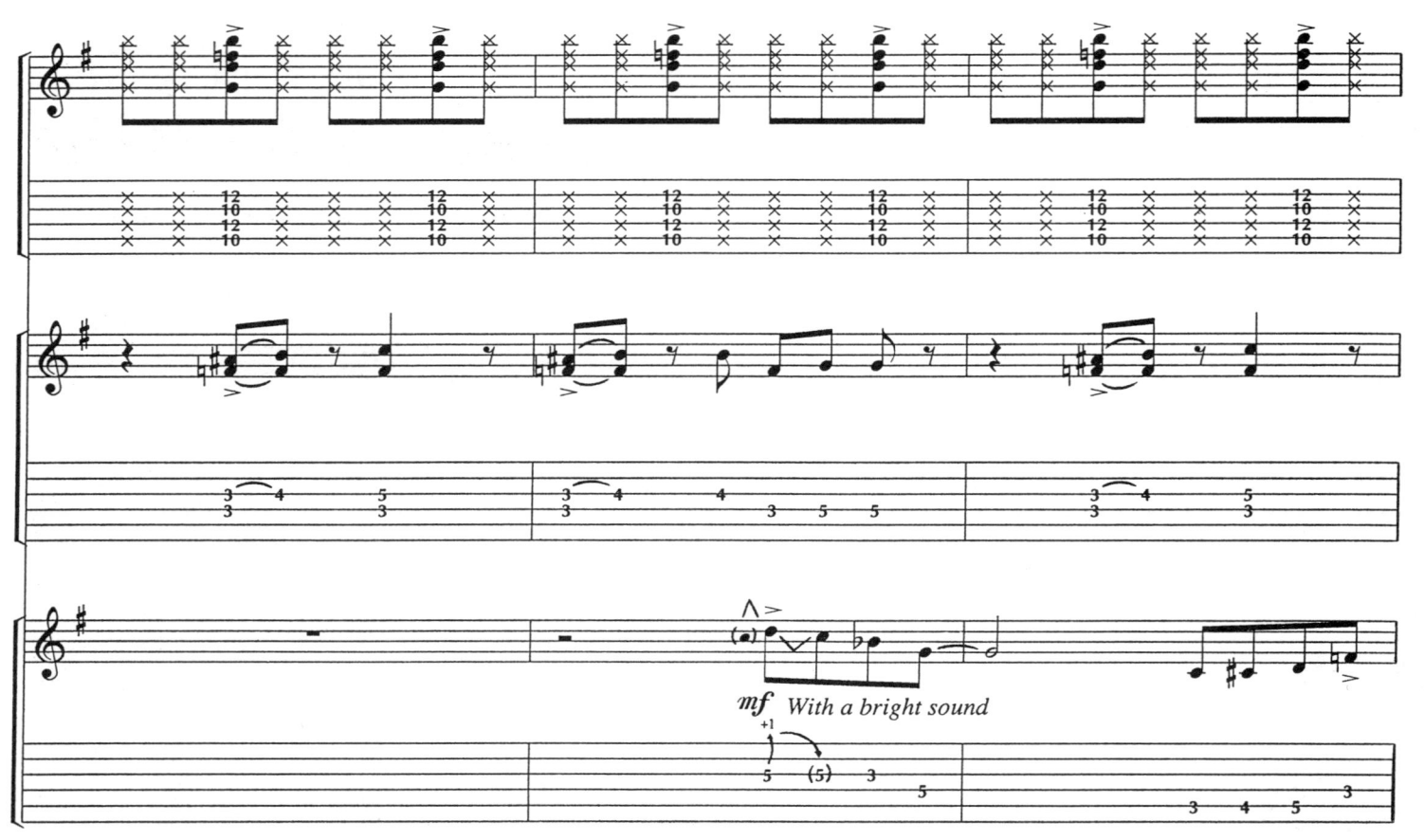

Cumberland Blues - 24 - 2

50

G7

I can't stay much long - er, Me - lin -

Cumberland Blues - 24 - 3

Cumberland Blues - 24 - 4

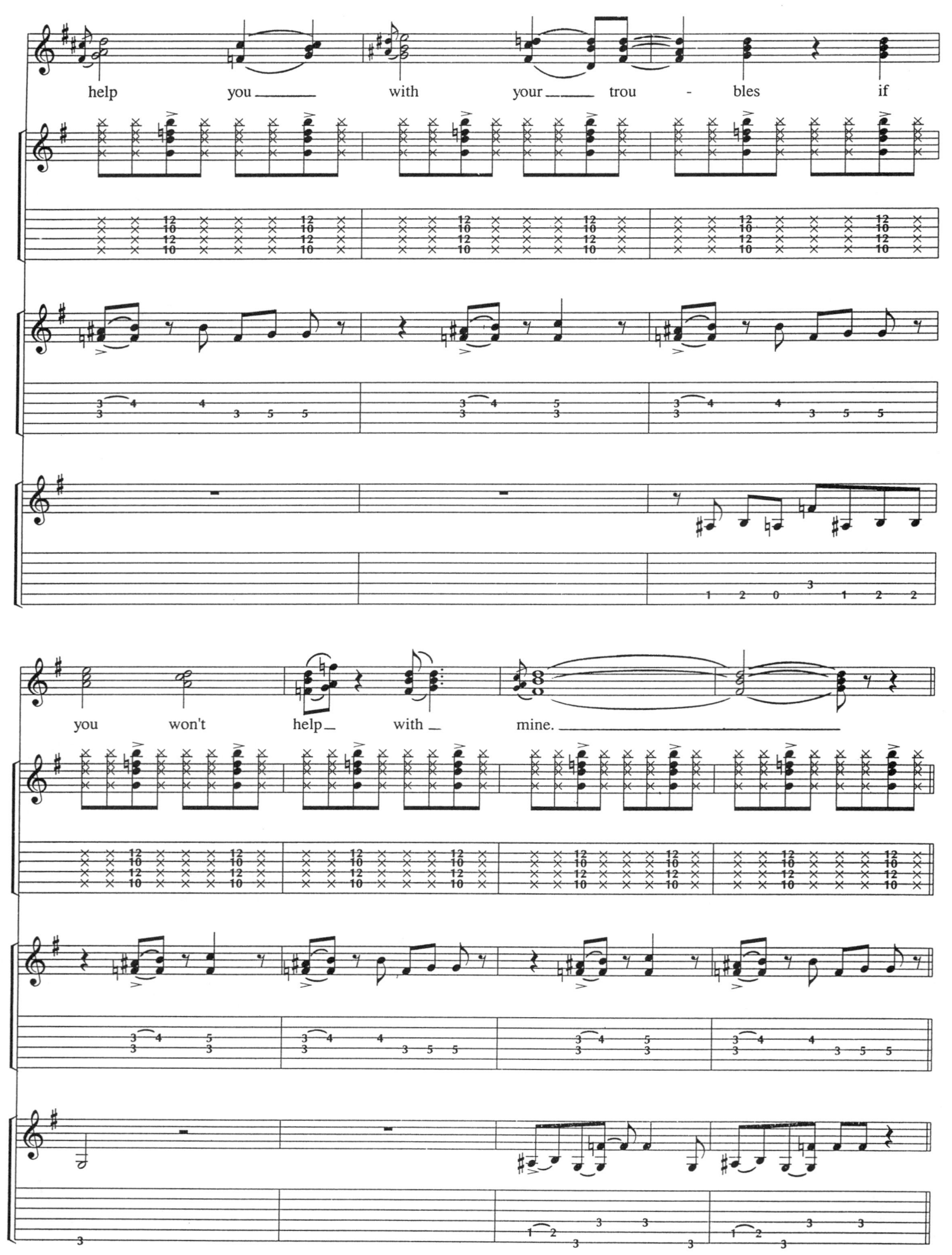

help you _____ with your _____ trou - bles if you won't help _ with _ mine. _____

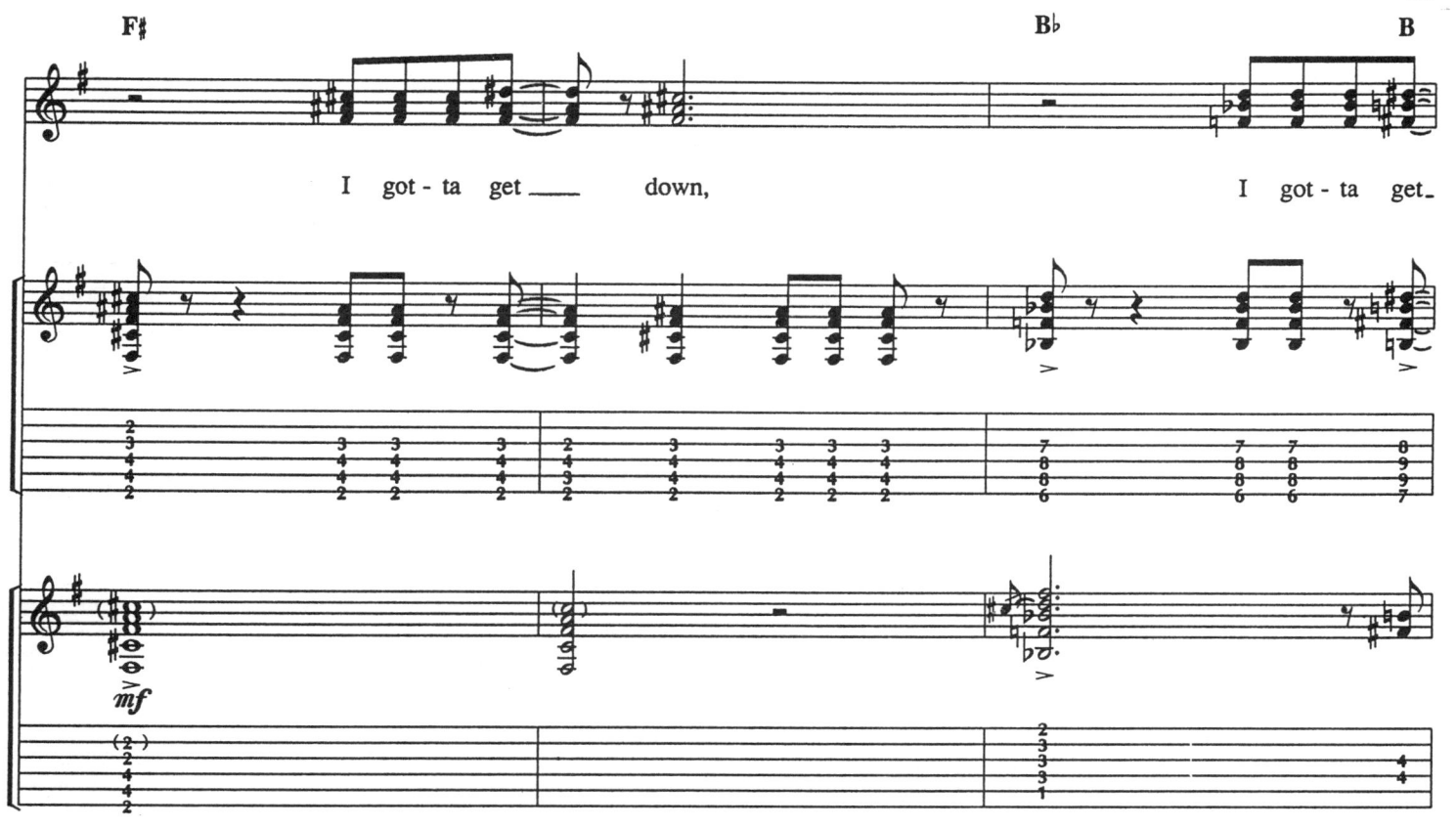

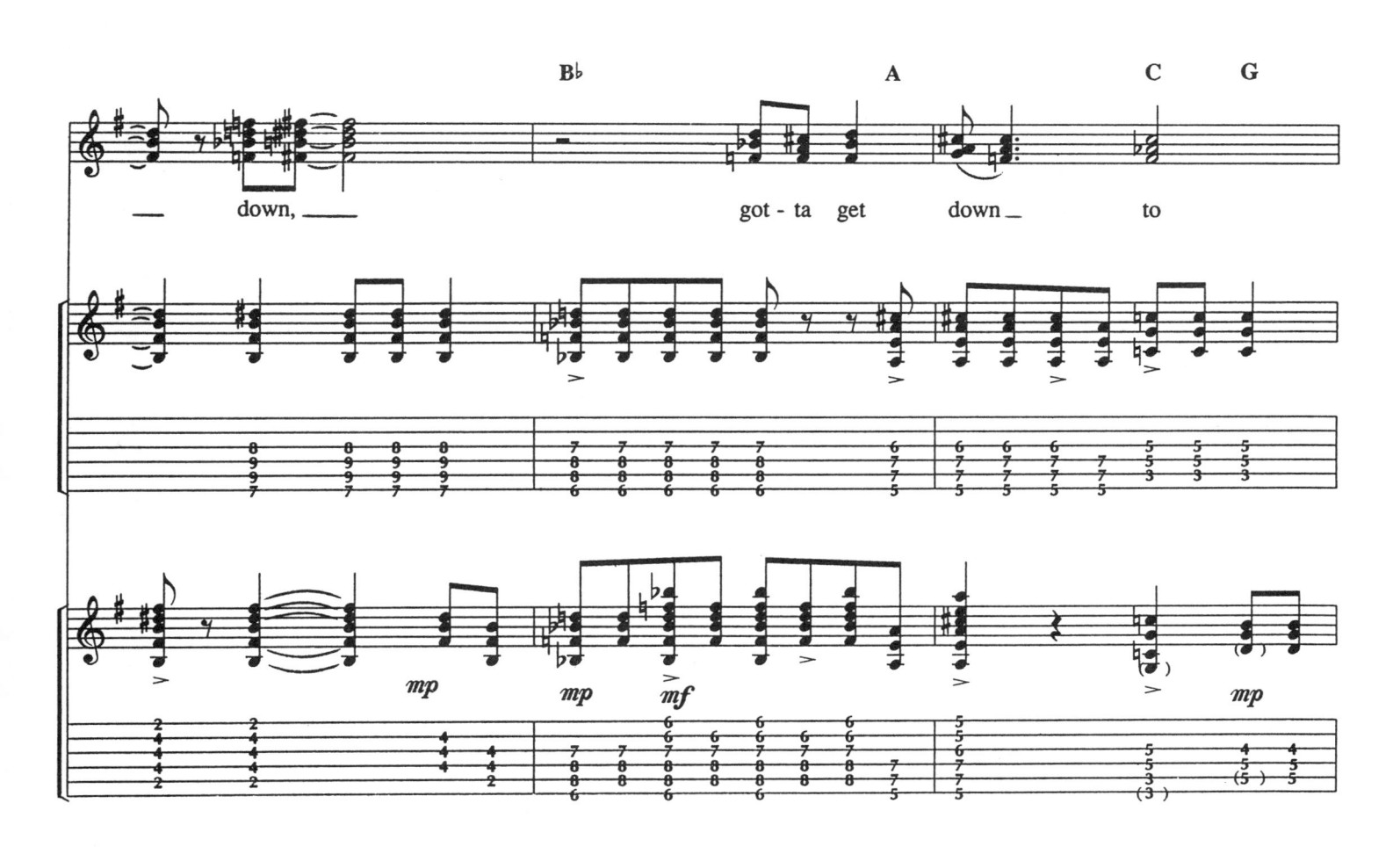

Lyrics:
I got-ta get ____ down, I got-ta get ____ down, ____ got-ta get down ____ to

Chords: F#, B♭, B, B♭, A, C, G

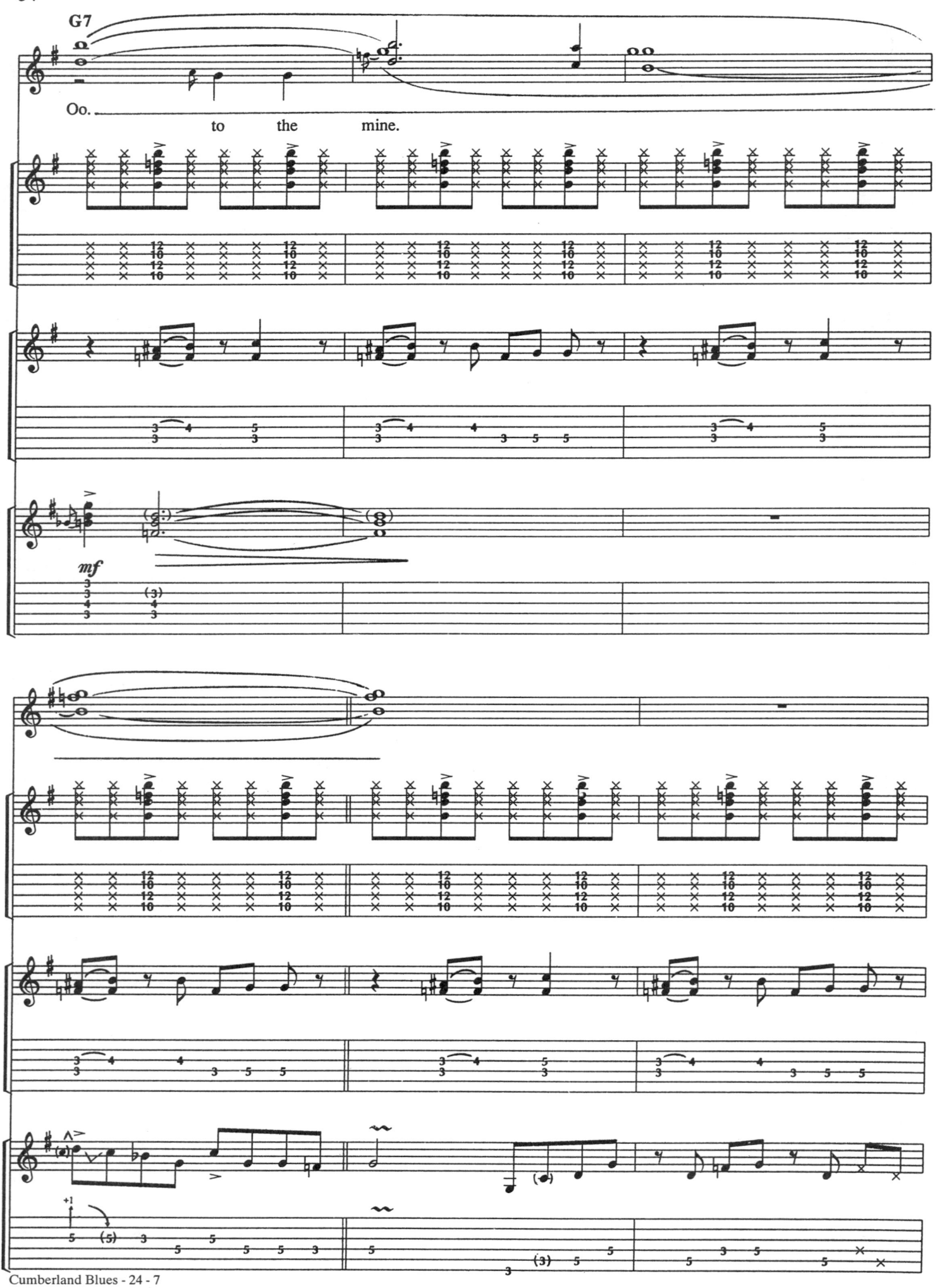

54

G7

Oo.   to   the   mine.

Cumberland Blues - 24 - 7

Cumberland Blues - 24 - 8

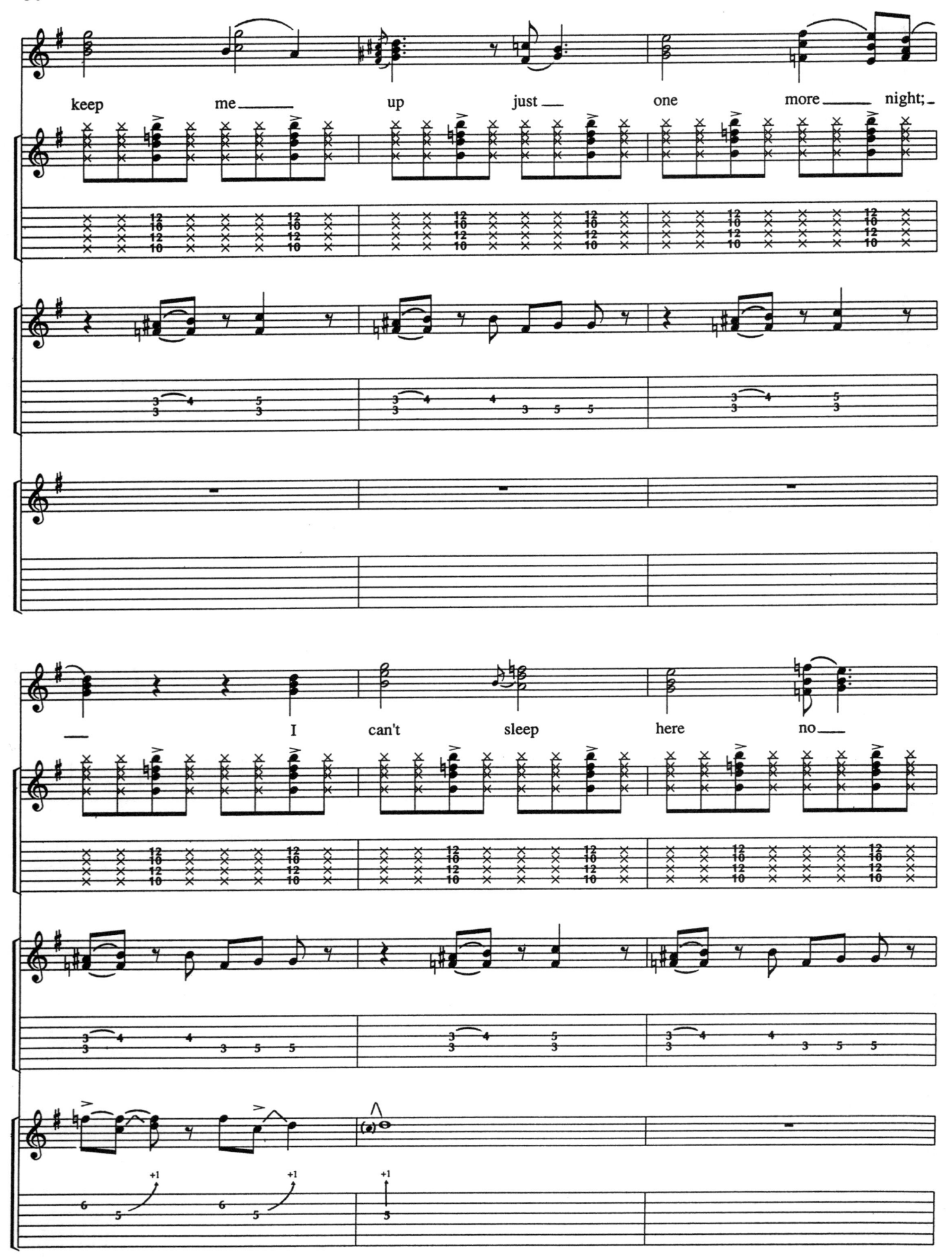

keep me up just one more night;

I can't sleep here no

Cumberland Blues - 24 - 9

more. _____ Lit- tle Ben _____

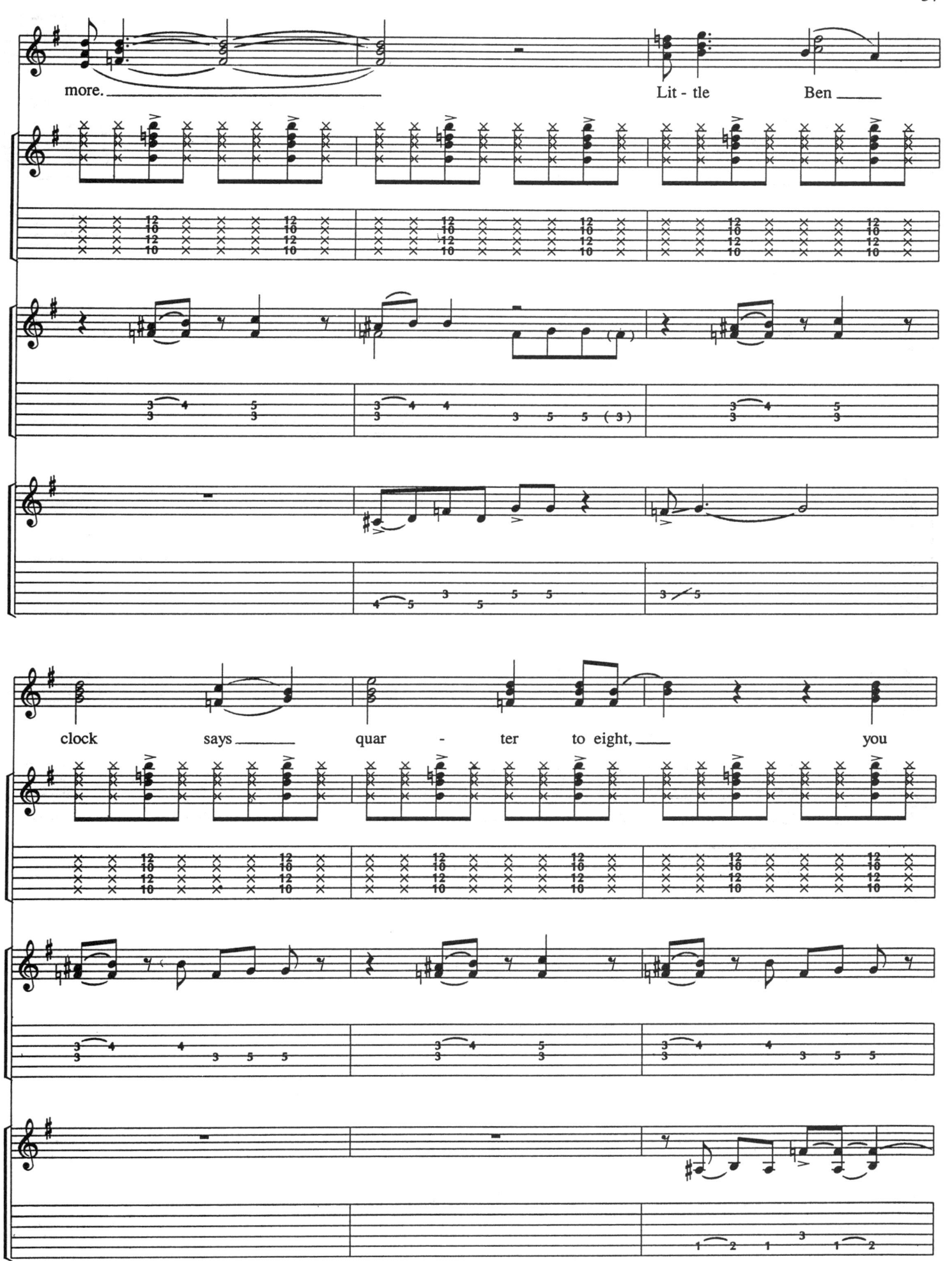

clock says _____ quar- ter to eight, _____ you

58

kept me up 'til four.

F#

I got-ta get down,

Cumberland Blues - 24 - 11

59

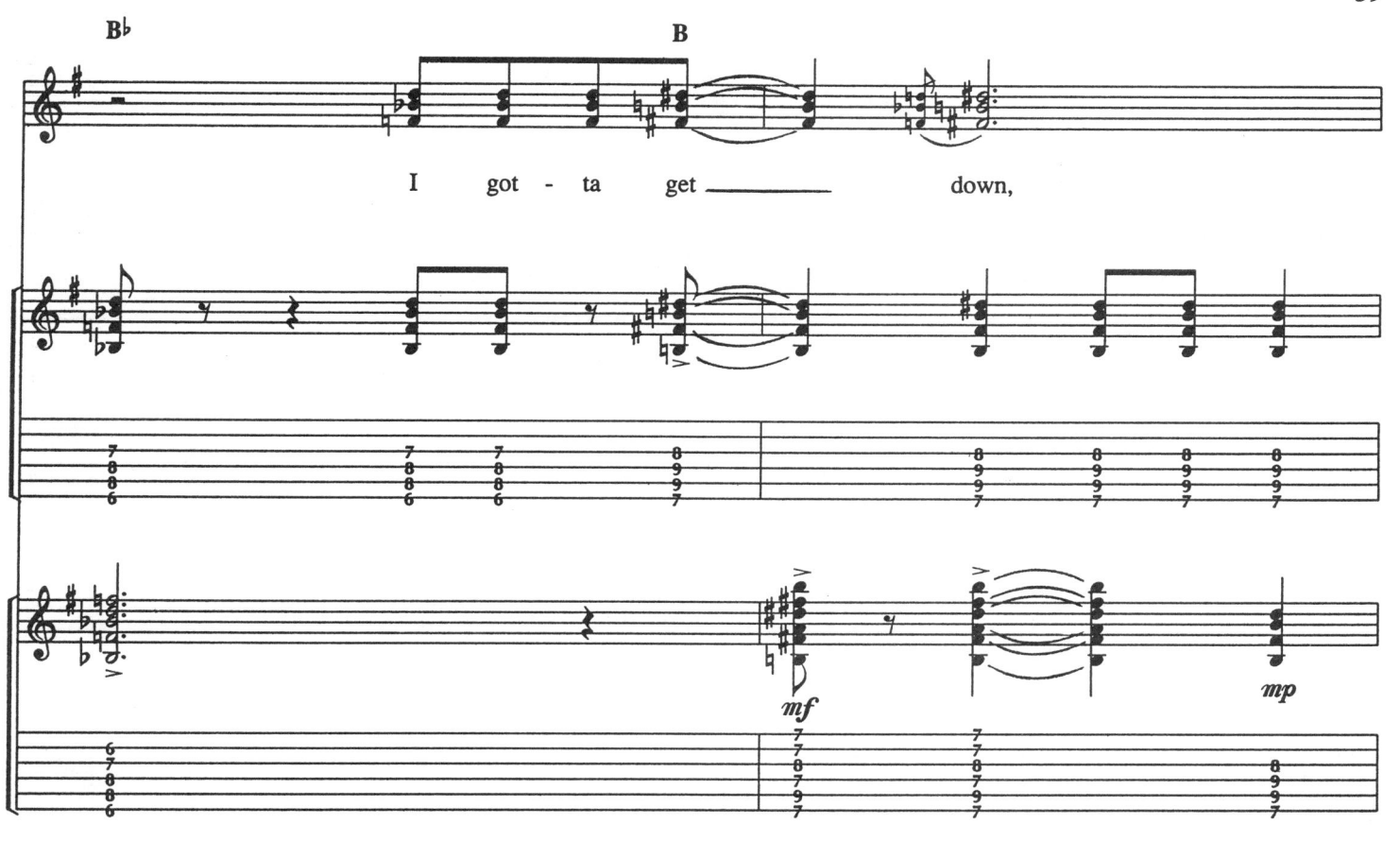

Lyrics: I got-ta get _____ down, or I can't work there no _____ more. _____

Chord symbols: B♭, B, B♭, A, A♭, G, G7

Cumberland Blues - 24 - 12

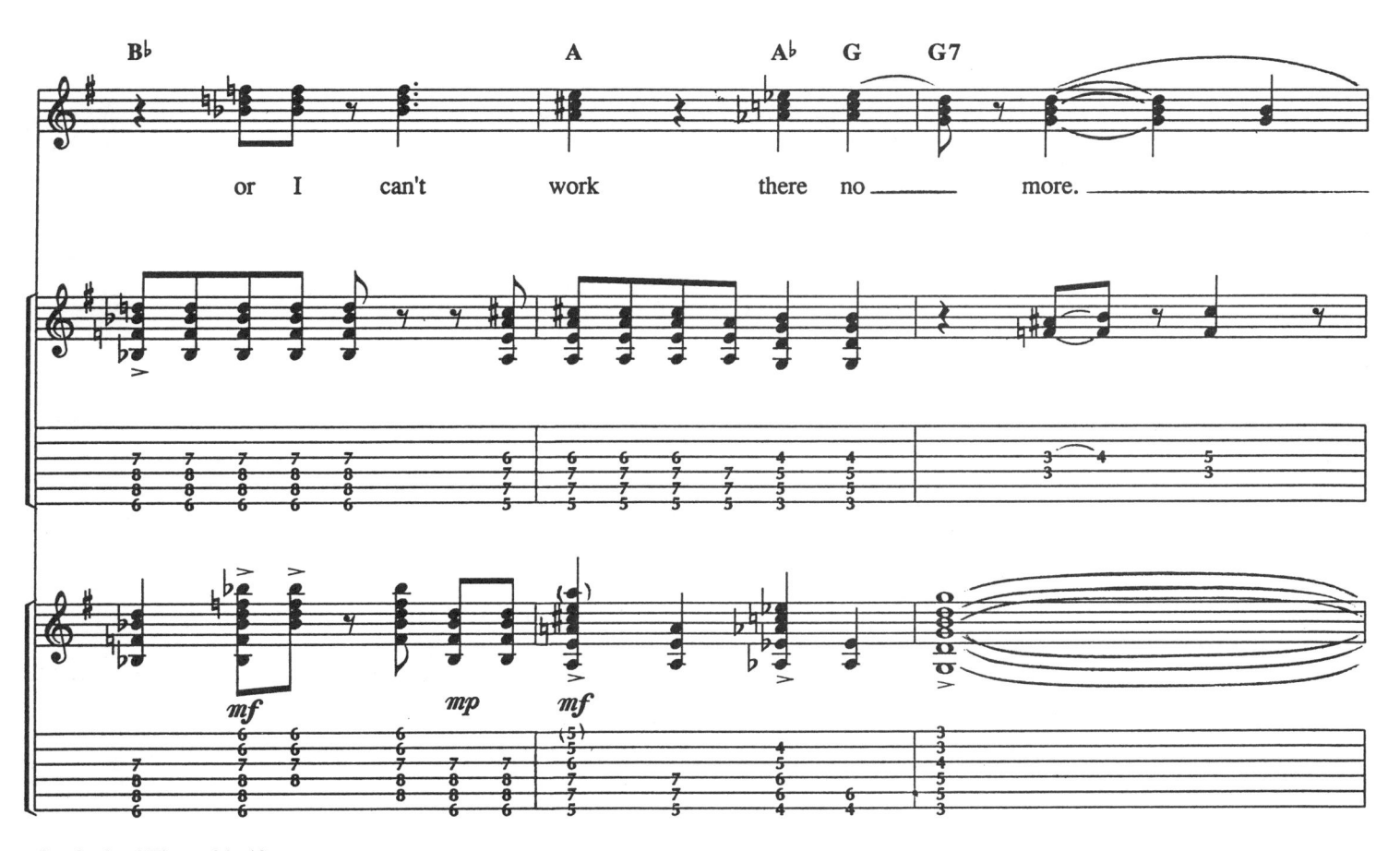

60

Cumberland Blues - 24 - 13

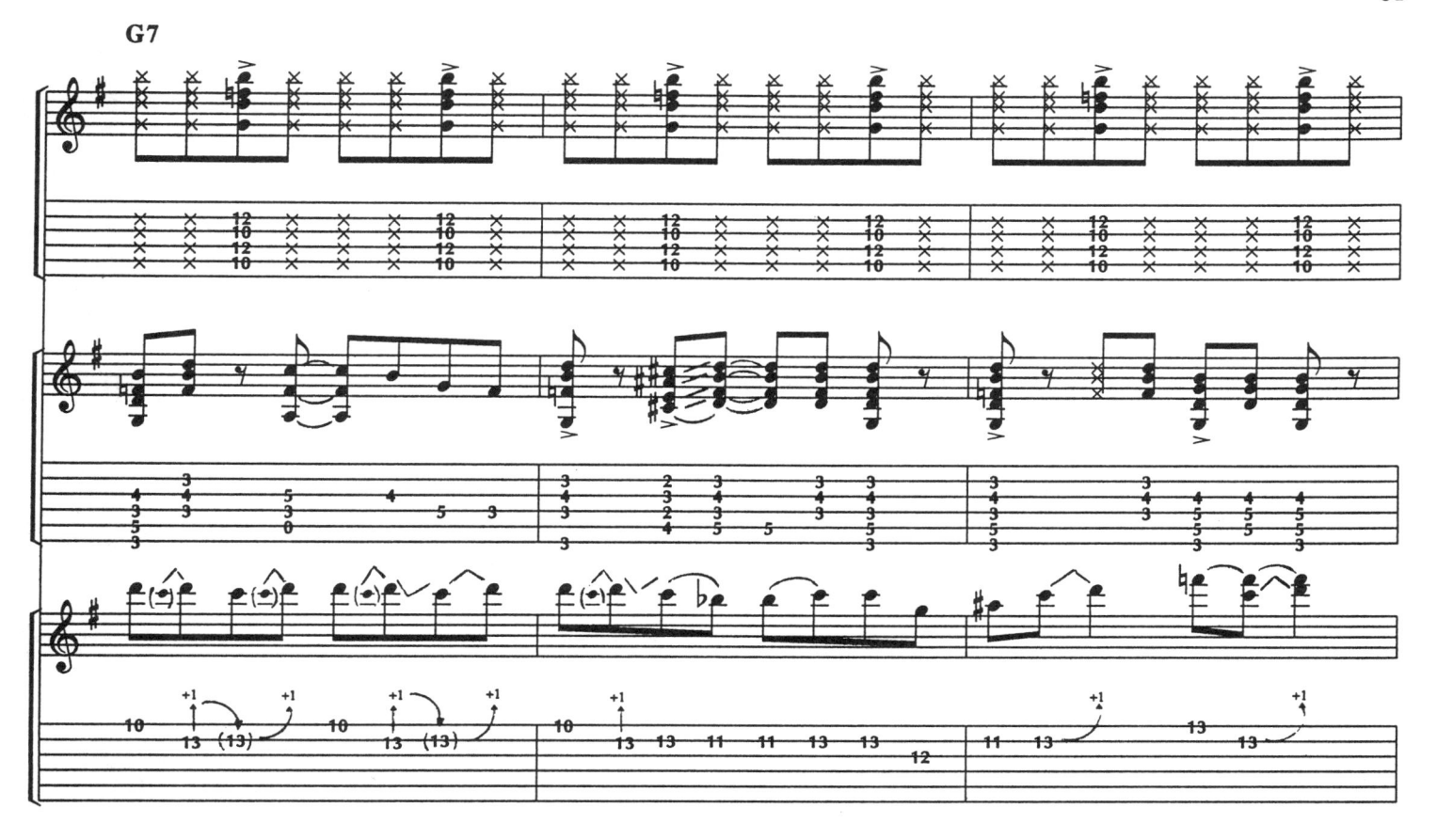

61

Cumberland Blues - 24 - 14

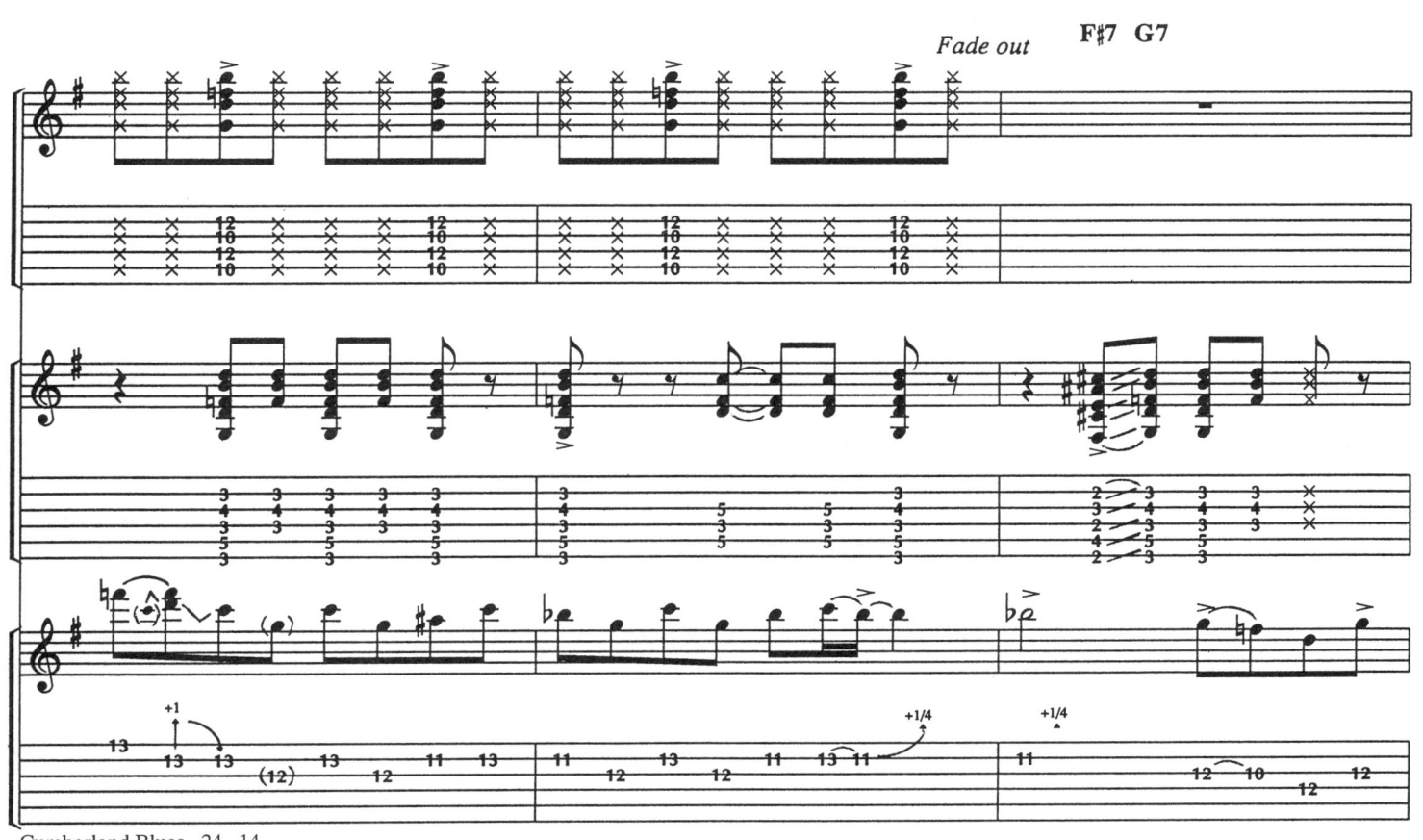

Cumberland Blues - 24 - 15

Cumberland Blues - 24 - 16

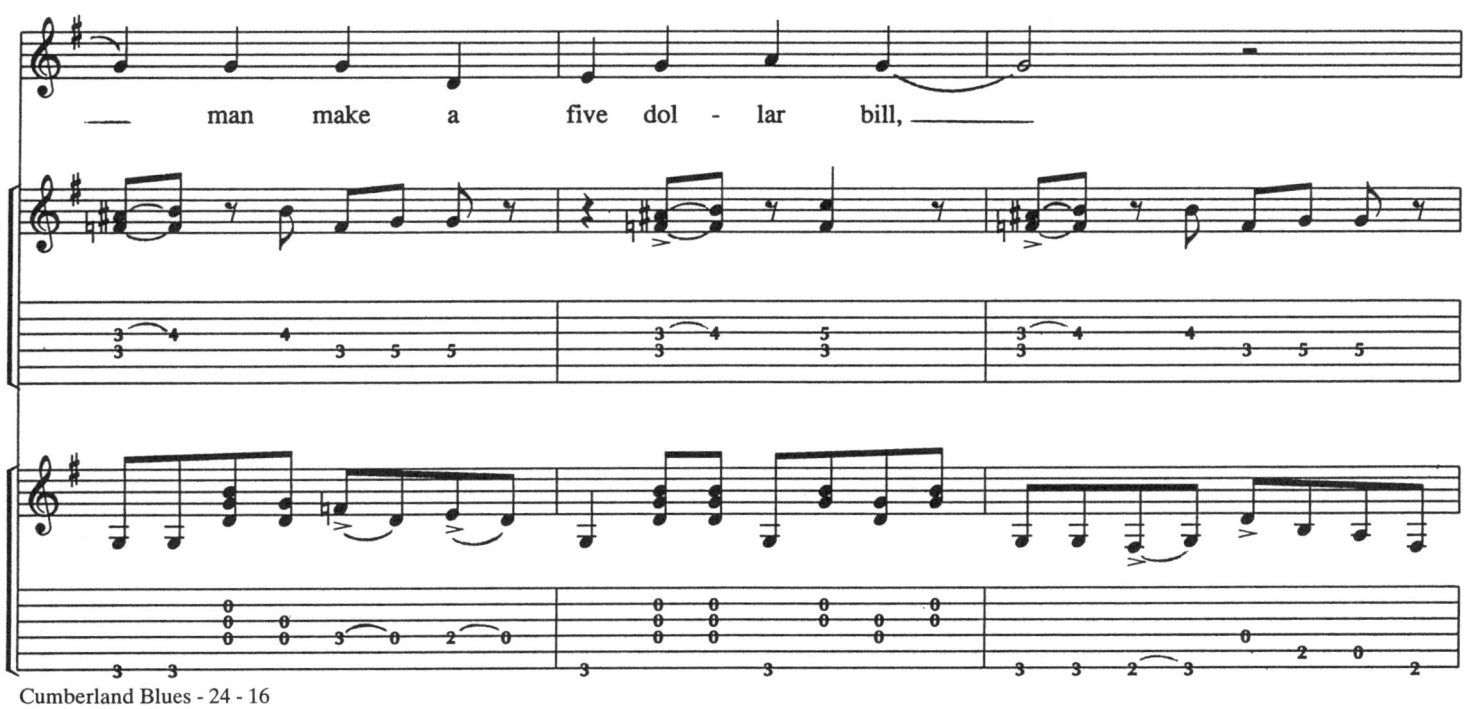

will keep him hap - py all the time.
Fade out
G
Some oth - er fel- lows mak - ing
G7
noth - ing at all
and you can
Guitar 4

hear him cry

Enter Banjo

Can I go, Bud-dy, can I go down, take your shift at the mine? Got-ta get down to the

Let ring

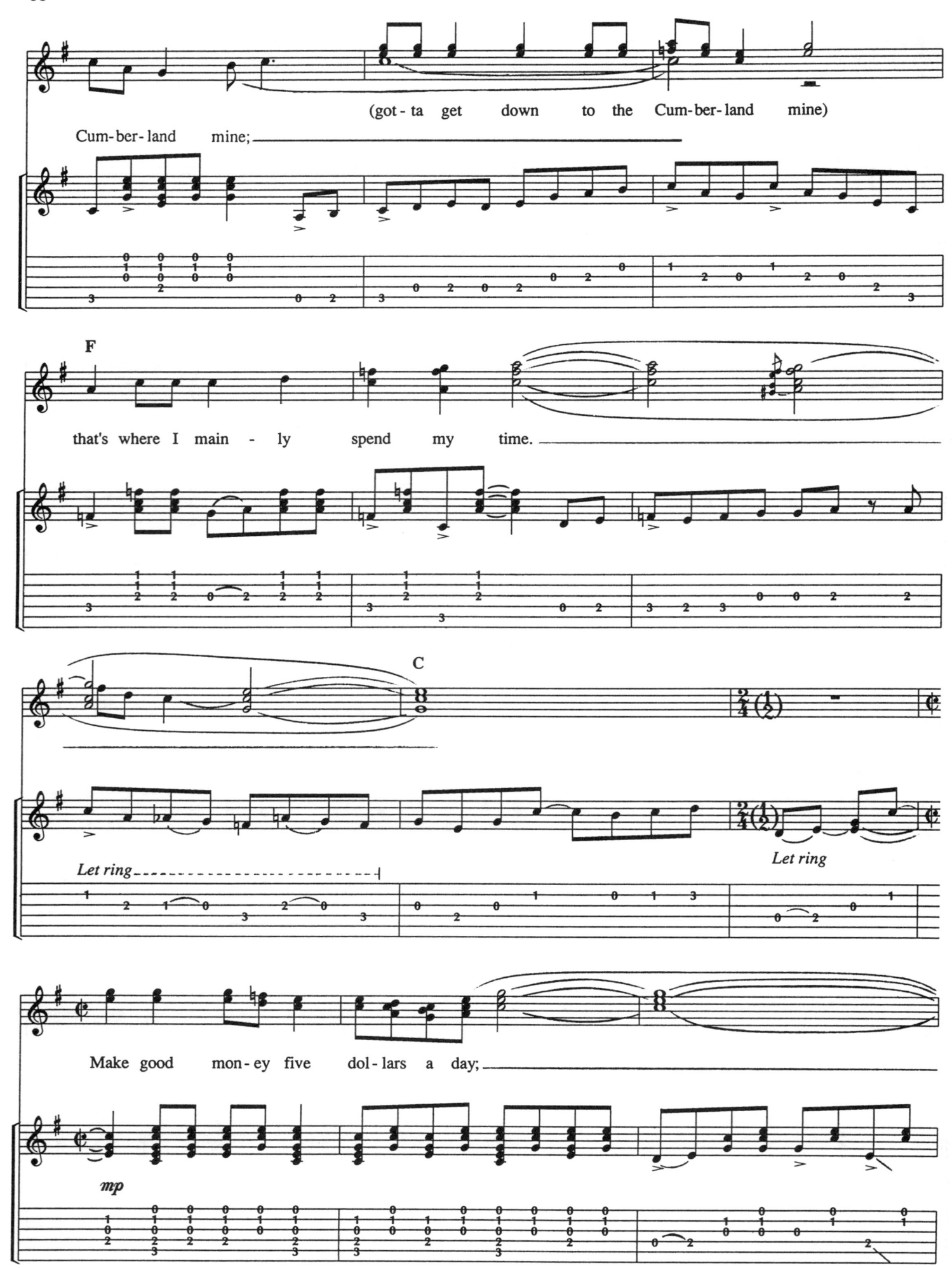

66

(got-ta get down to the Cum-ber-land mine)
Cum-ber-land mine;

F
that's where I main-ly spend my time.

C

Let ring   Let ring

Make good mon-ey five dol-lars a day;

mp

Cumberland Blues - 24 - 19

made an-y more I might move a-way.

Lot-ta poor man got the Cum-ber-land blues; he can't win for los-ing. Lot-ta the poor man got to walk the line

Cumberland Blues - 24 - 21

just to pay his union dues.

I don't know now, I just don't know if I'm going back again.

I don't know now, I just don't

(Fade in)

Cumberland Blues - 24 - 22

know _____ if I'm go-ing back __ a-gain. __

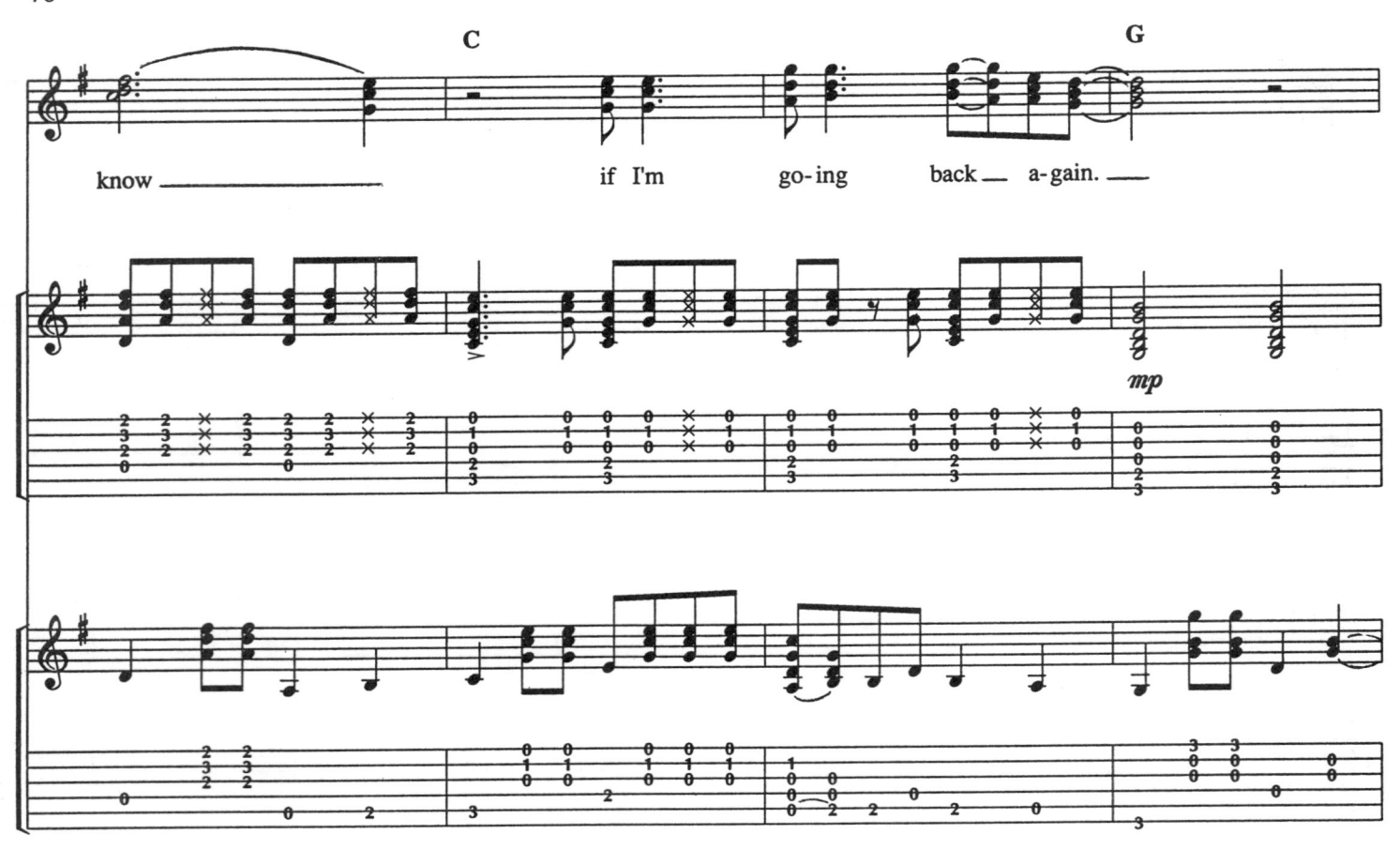

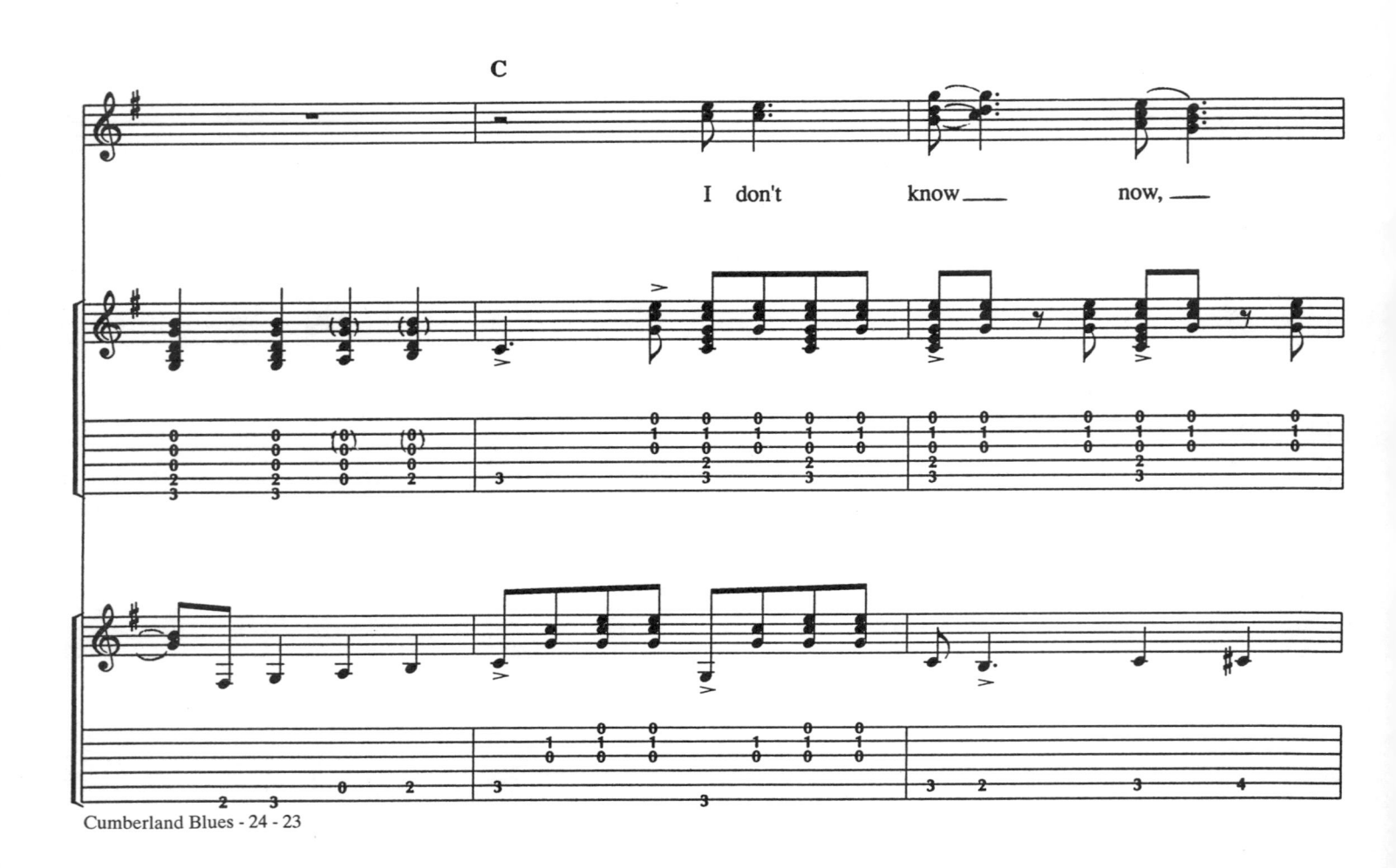

I don't know __ now, __

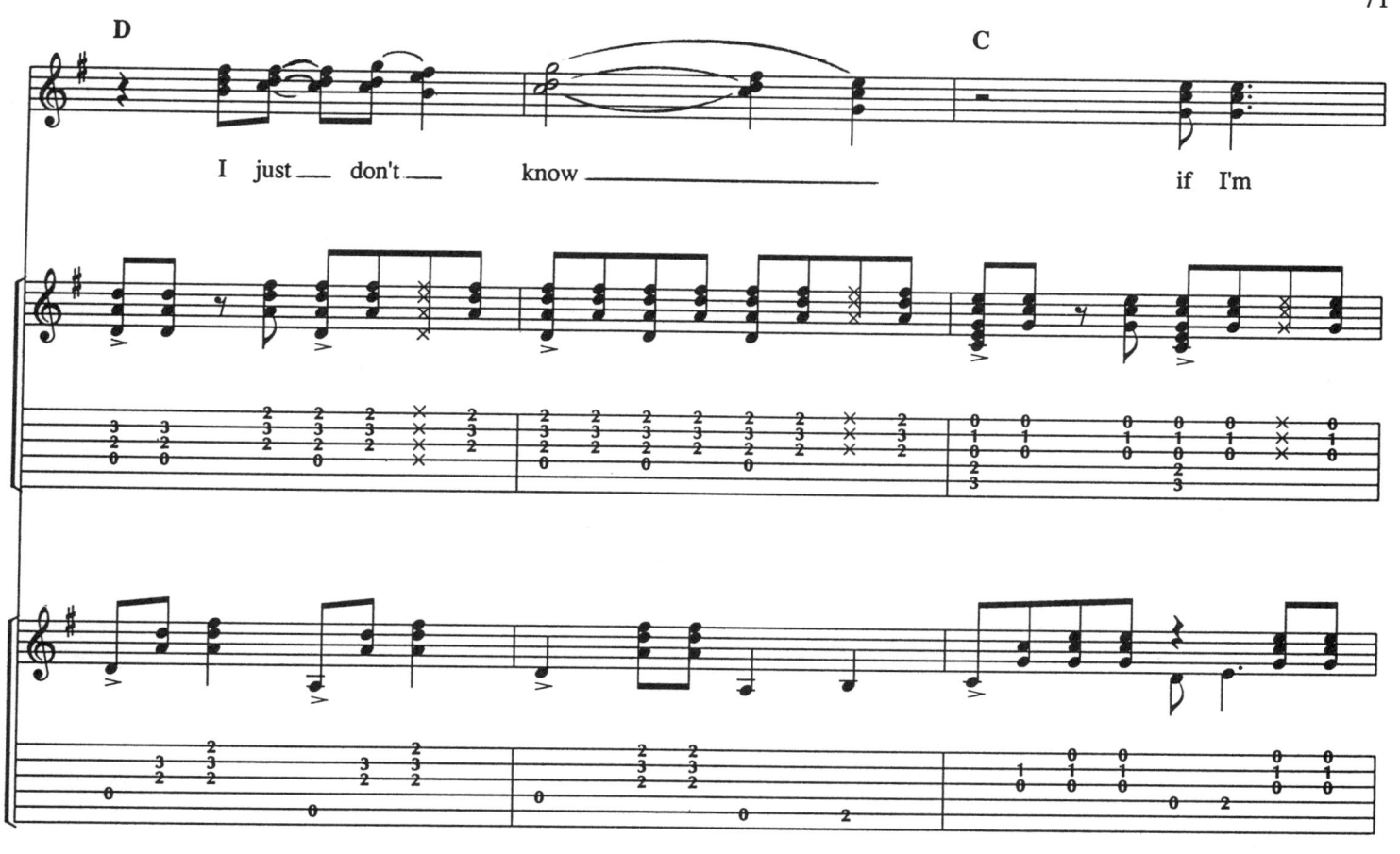

71

I just don't know ⸺ if I'm going back a-gain.

Cumberland Blues - 24 - 24

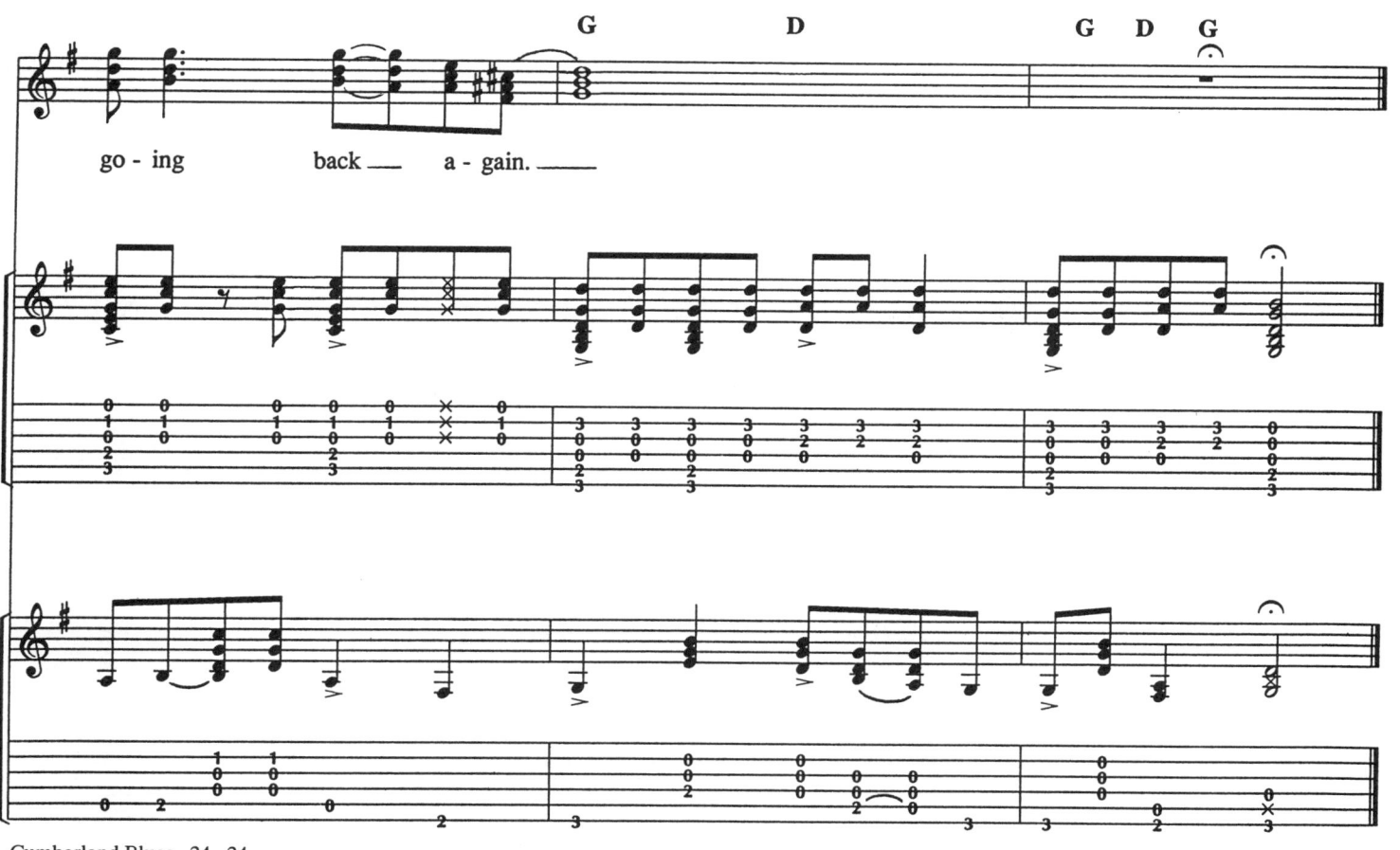

BLACK PETER

Words by ROBERT HUNTER
Music by JERRY GARCIA

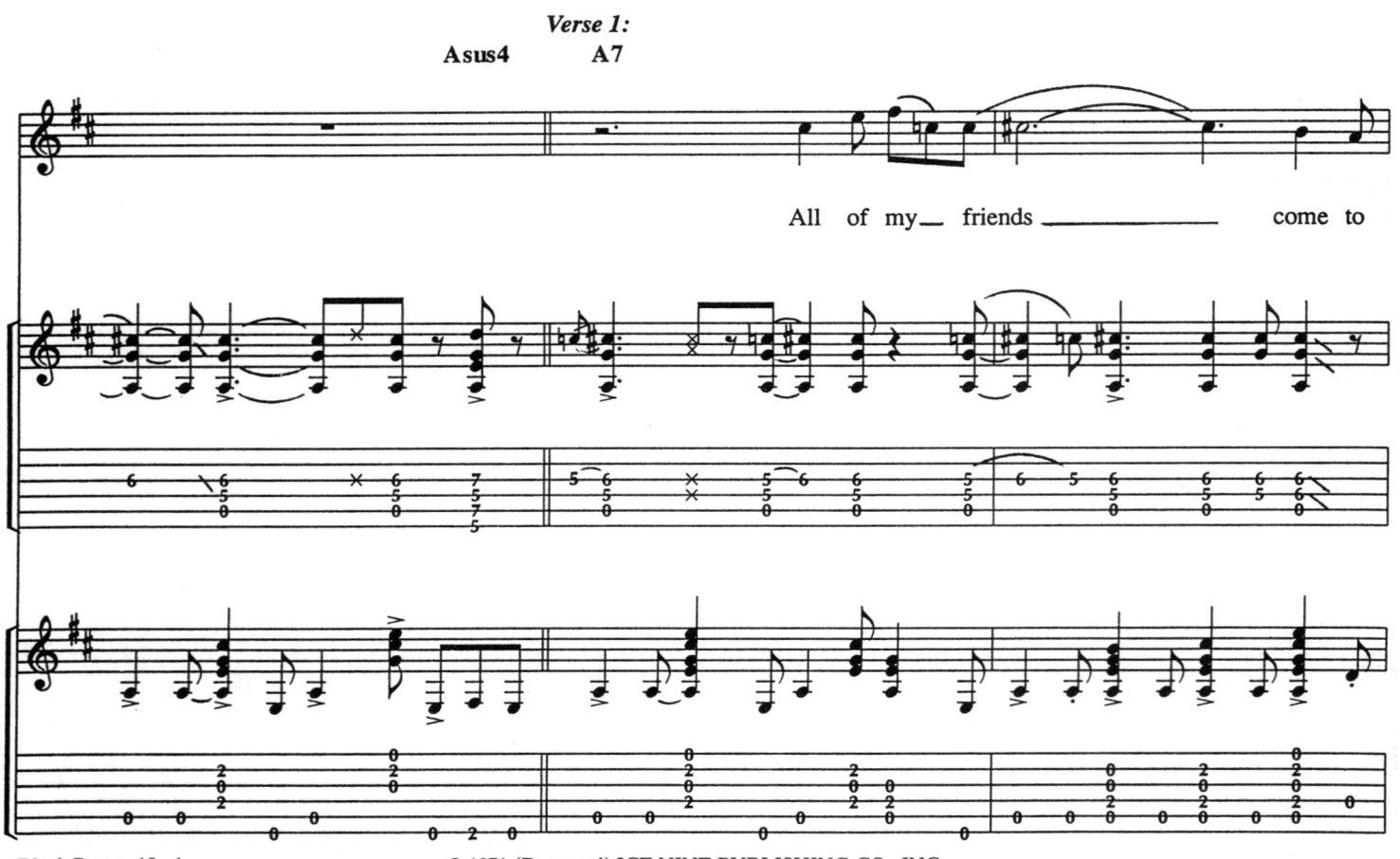

Moderately slow Blues

Intro:

Verse 1:

All of my friends come to

D7
A7
see me last night.
I was lay-
Asus4
D7
D7(addE)
ing in my bed and dy - ing.
mp

74

Lyrics: An - nie Beu - neau ___ from Saint ___ An - gel ___ say the ___ weath - er down here ___

Chords: Em | Bm | A | G | F#m | Em

so fine.

Verse 2:

Just then the wind came squalling through the door, but who can the weather command?___ Just wan-na have___

*Tap guitar body   Let ring

___ a lit-tle peace___ to ___ die, ___ and a___

Let ring

Black Peter - 19 - 6

friend_ or two_ I love_ at hand._

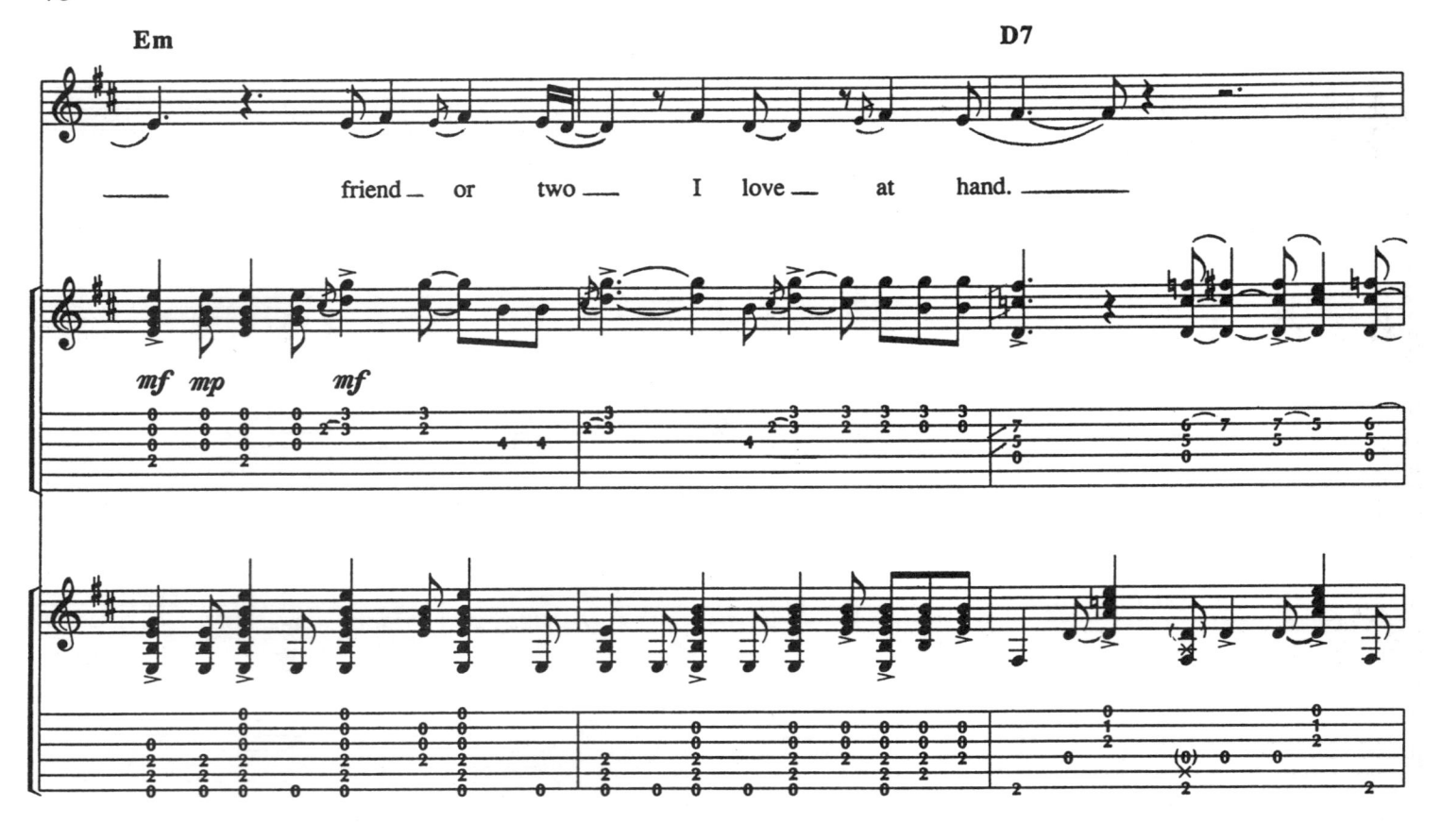

Fev - er roll up to a hun-dred and five

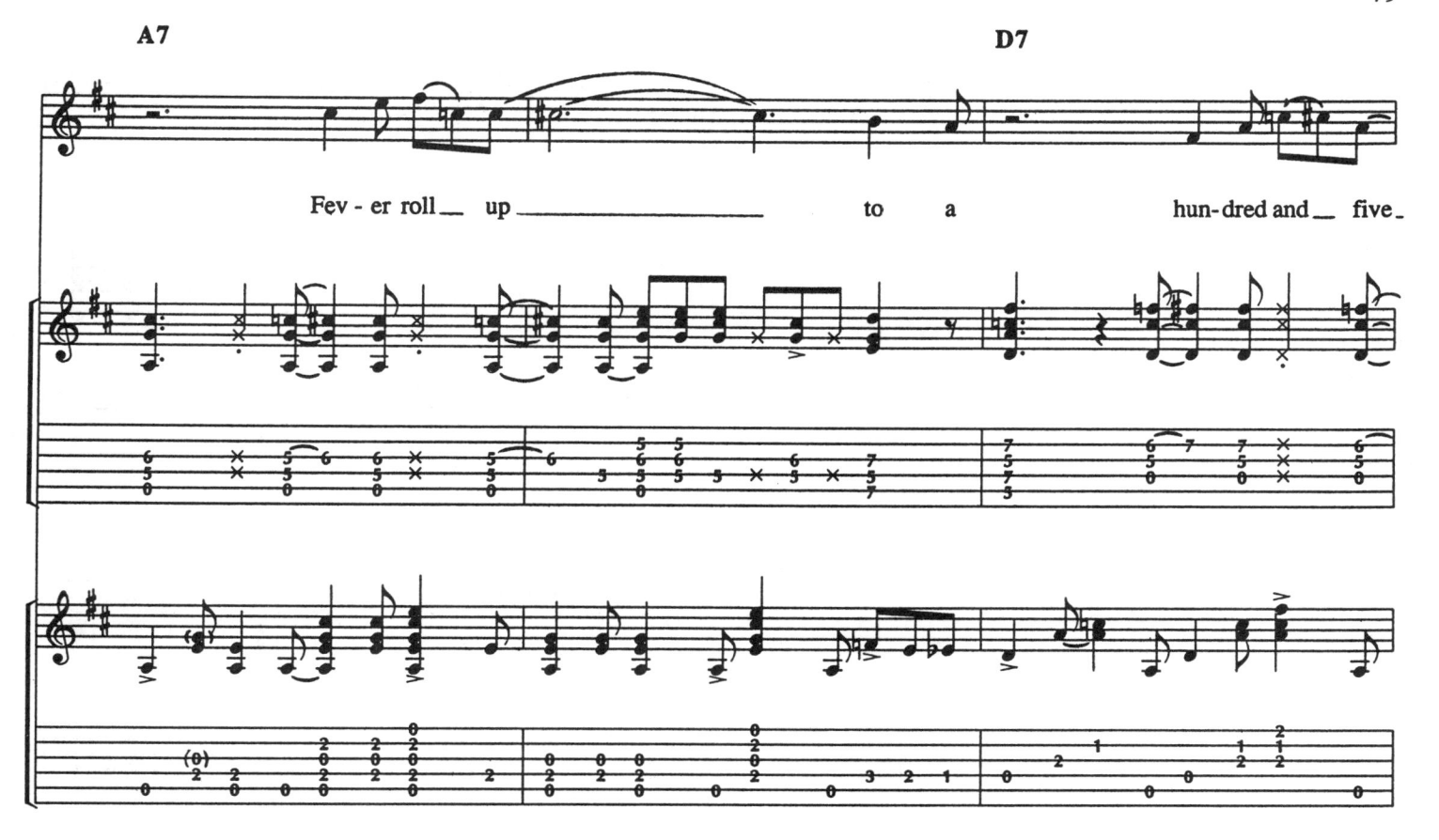

Roll on up, gon-na roll back

Black Peter - 19 - 8

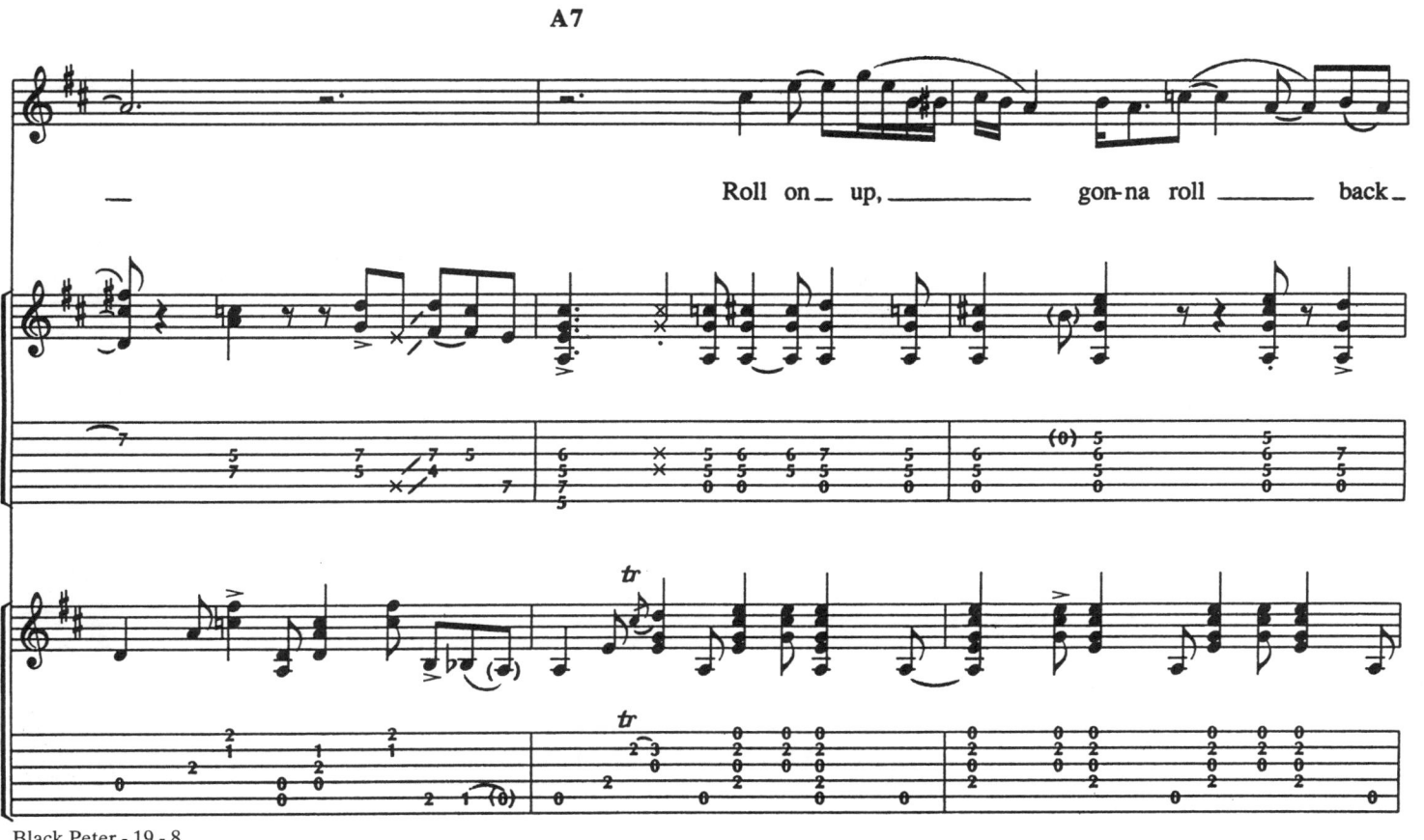

down. — One more day — down — I find myself alive, tomorrow may-be go_ be-neath the ground._

Let ring

Gradual cresc.

Black Peter - 19 - 10

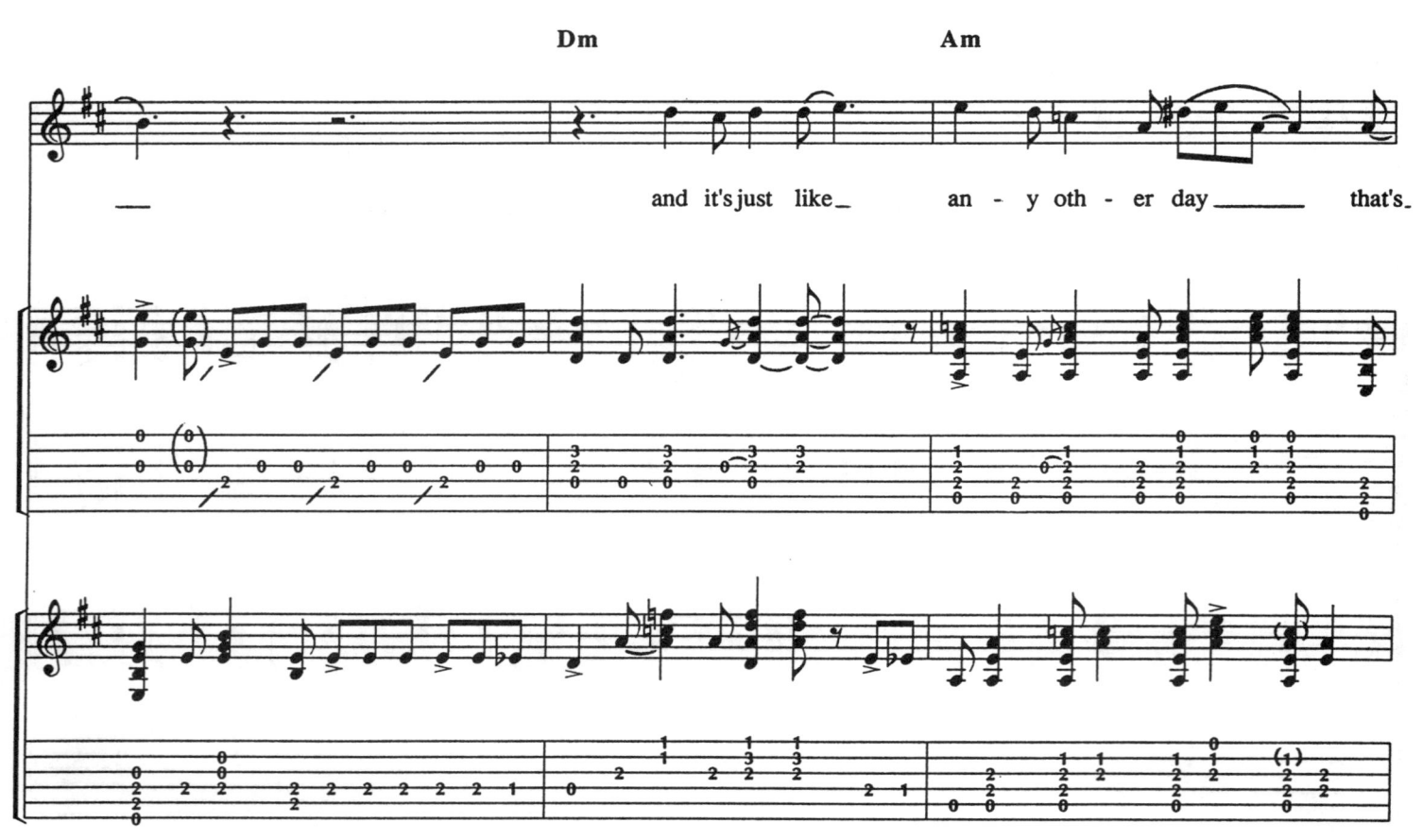

See here how ev-'ry thing lead up to this day, and it's just like an-y oth-er day that's ev - er been. Sun going up and then the sun go - ing down.

Black Peter - 19 - 12

Shine ____ thru my win-dow ____ and my friends ____ they come ____ a-round, ____ come a - round ____ a-

Black Peter - 19 - 13

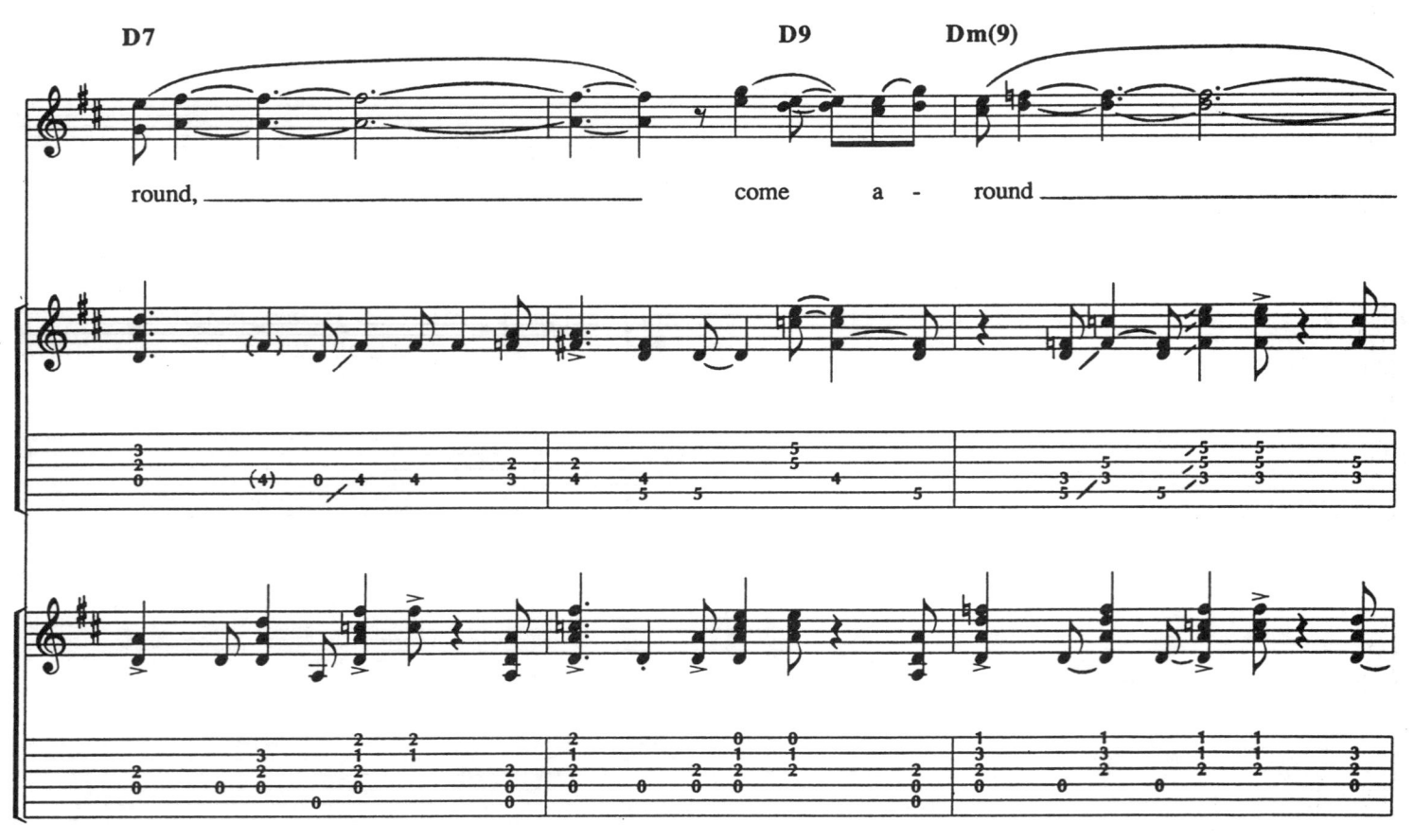

come a-round. Ah.

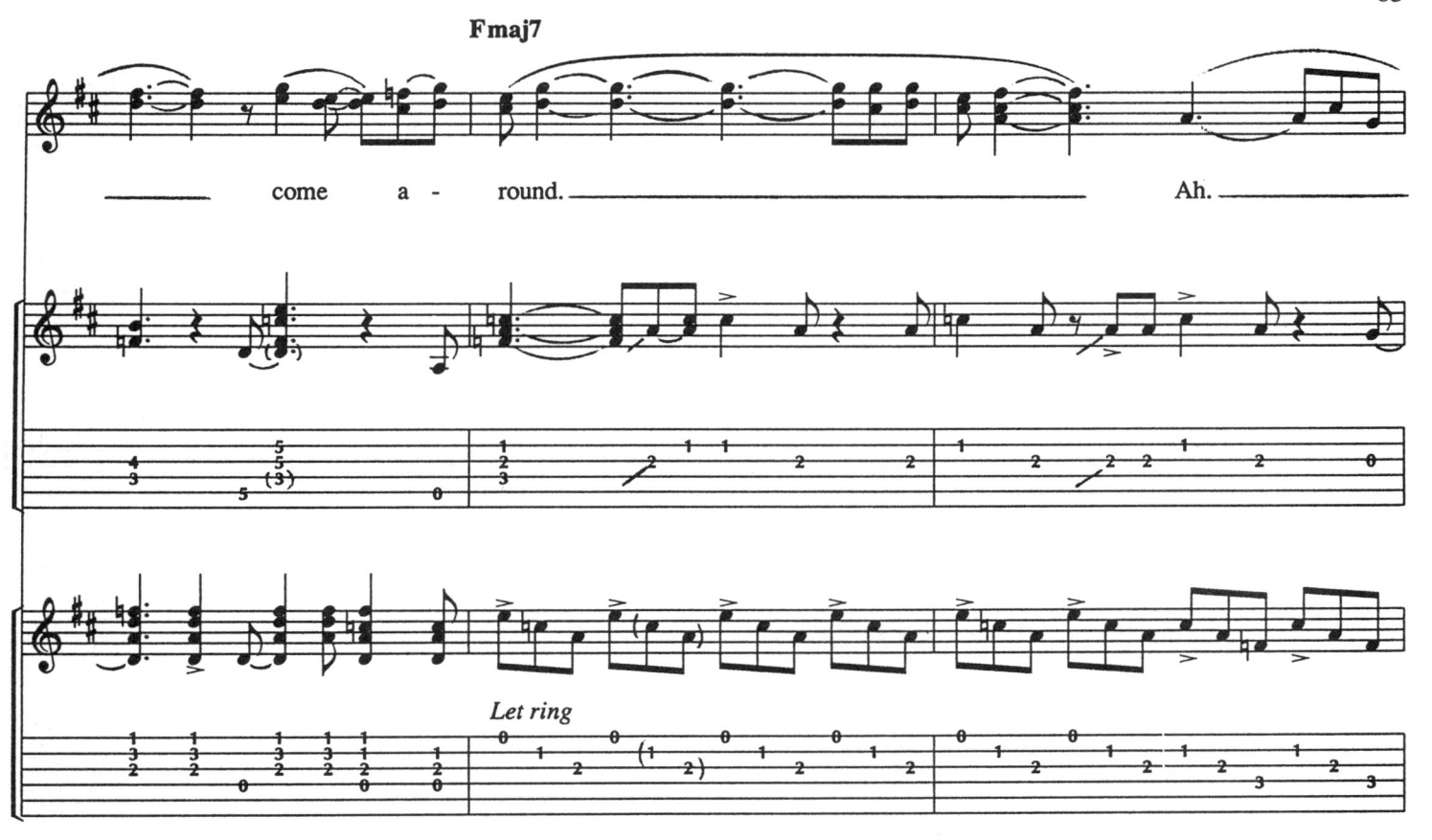

Verse 4:

The peo-ple may know, but the peo-ple don't care that a man can be as poor as

Black Peter - 19 - 15

me. Take a look at poor Pe-ter; he's lying in pain.

88

Em | Em7 | Em6

Now let's go run and see.

D7

Run and see,

Let ring

Black Peter - 19 - 17

run ____ and ____ see, ____

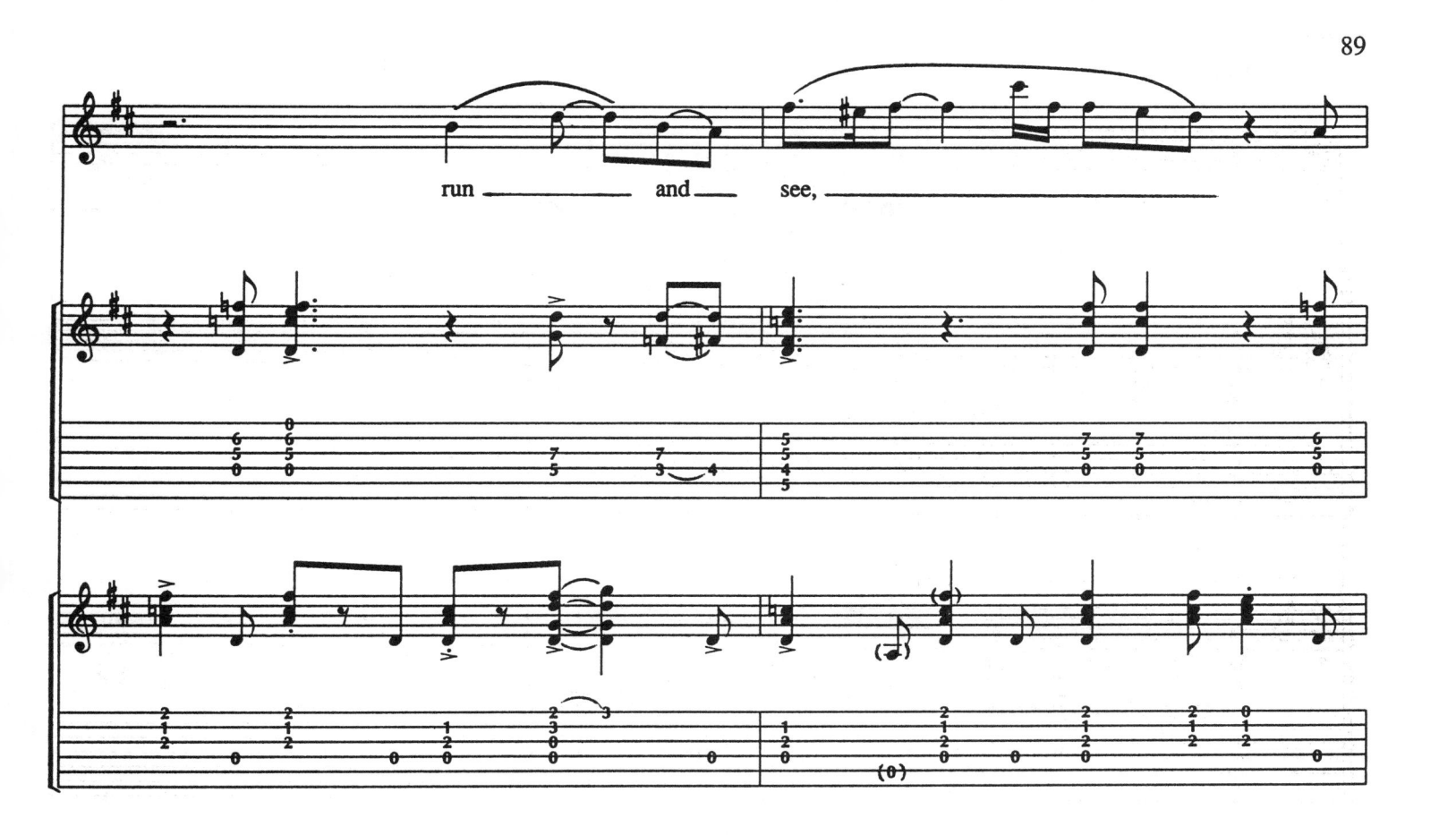

run, ____ run and see ____ run and

see.

EASY WIND

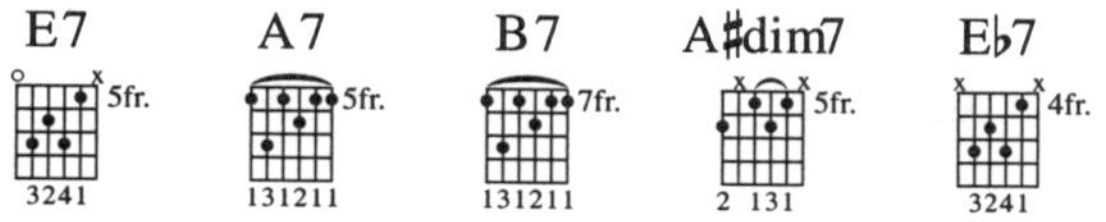

Words and Music by
ROBERT HUNTER

Moderately ♩ = 86

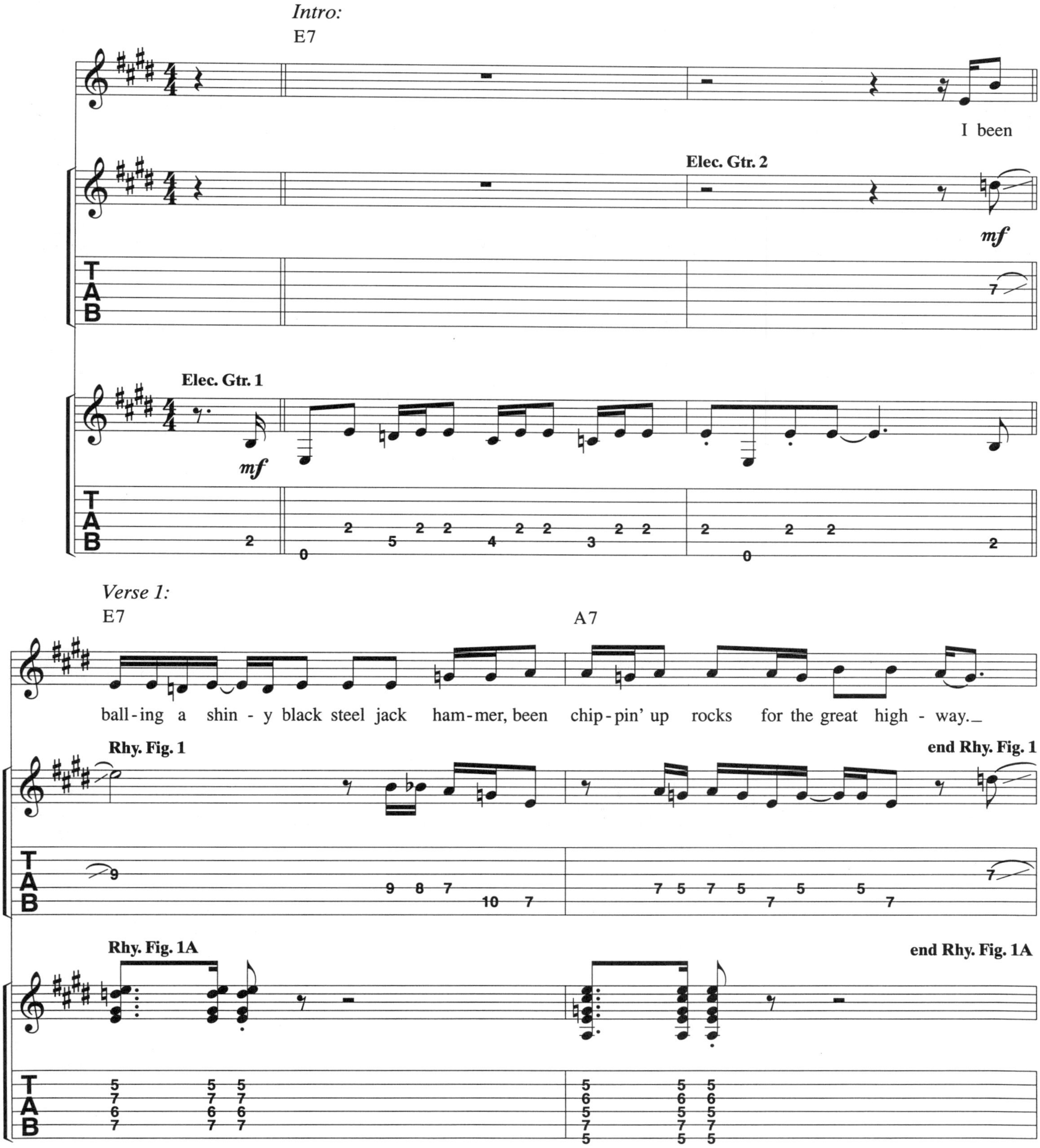

w/Rhy. Figs. 1 *(Elec. Gtr. 2)* **& 1A** *(Elec. Gtr. 1) both 3 times*

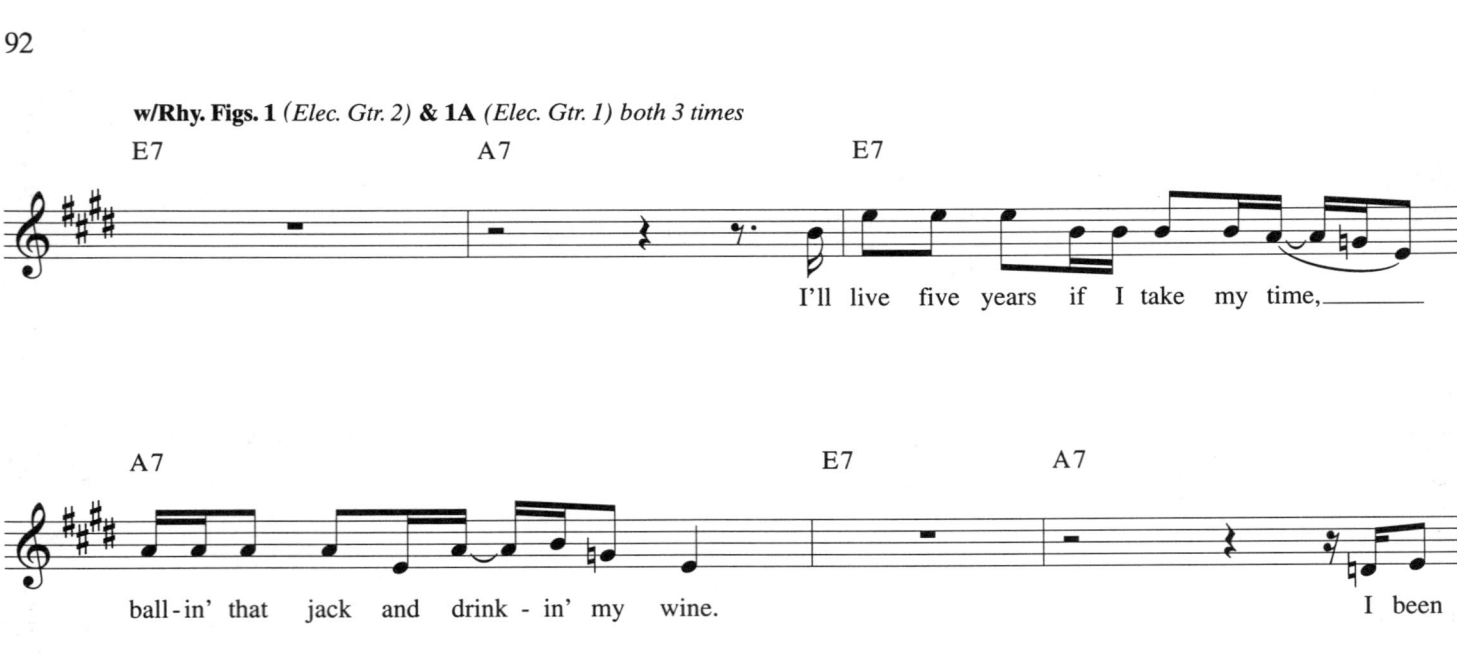

I'll live five years if I take my time,___

ball-in' that jack and drink-in' my wine. I been

Verse 2:
w/Rhy. Figs. 1 *(Elec. Gtr. 2)* **& 1A** *(Elec. Gtr. 1) both 2 times*

chip-pin' them rocks from dawn till doom while my rid-er hide my bot-tle in the oth-er room.___

Doc-tor say bet-ter stop ball-in' that jack, if I

Easy Wind - 11 - 2

live five years I'm gon-na bust my back,___ yes, I will.___

Chorus:

Eas - y wind___ 'cross the Bay - ou to - day,___

Easy Wind - 11 - 3

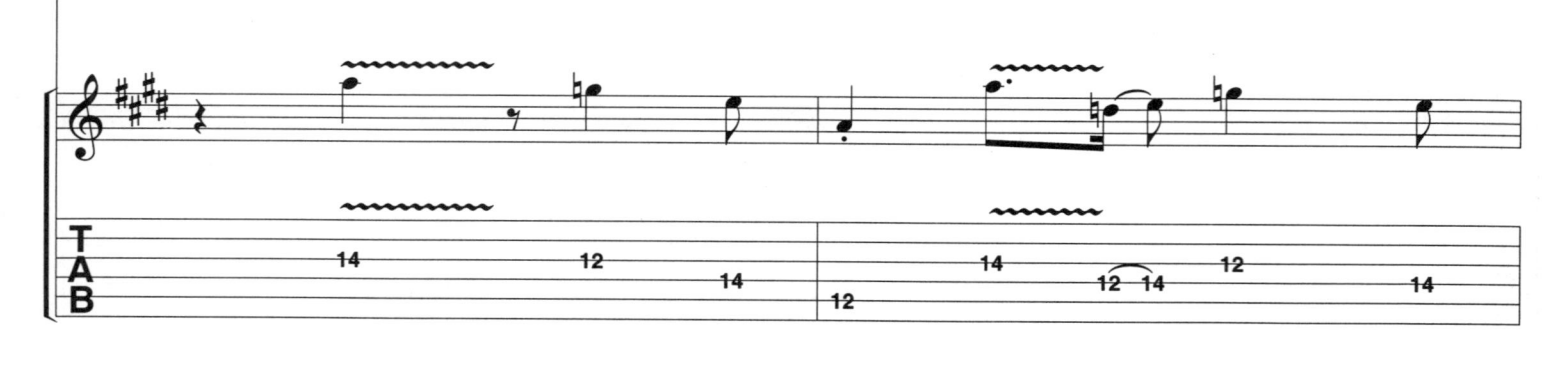

'cause there's a whole lotta wom-en, ma-ma, out in red on the streets to-day.

river keeps a-talkin', but you never heard a word it said.

96

Harmonica Solo:
w/Rhy. Figs. 1 *(Elec. Gtr. 2)* **& 1A** *(Elec. Gtr. 1) both simile*

Play 5 times

Guitar Solo:
w/Rhy. Fig. 1A *(Elec. Gtr. 1) 4 times simile*

Elec. Gtr. 2

Easy Wind - 11 - 6

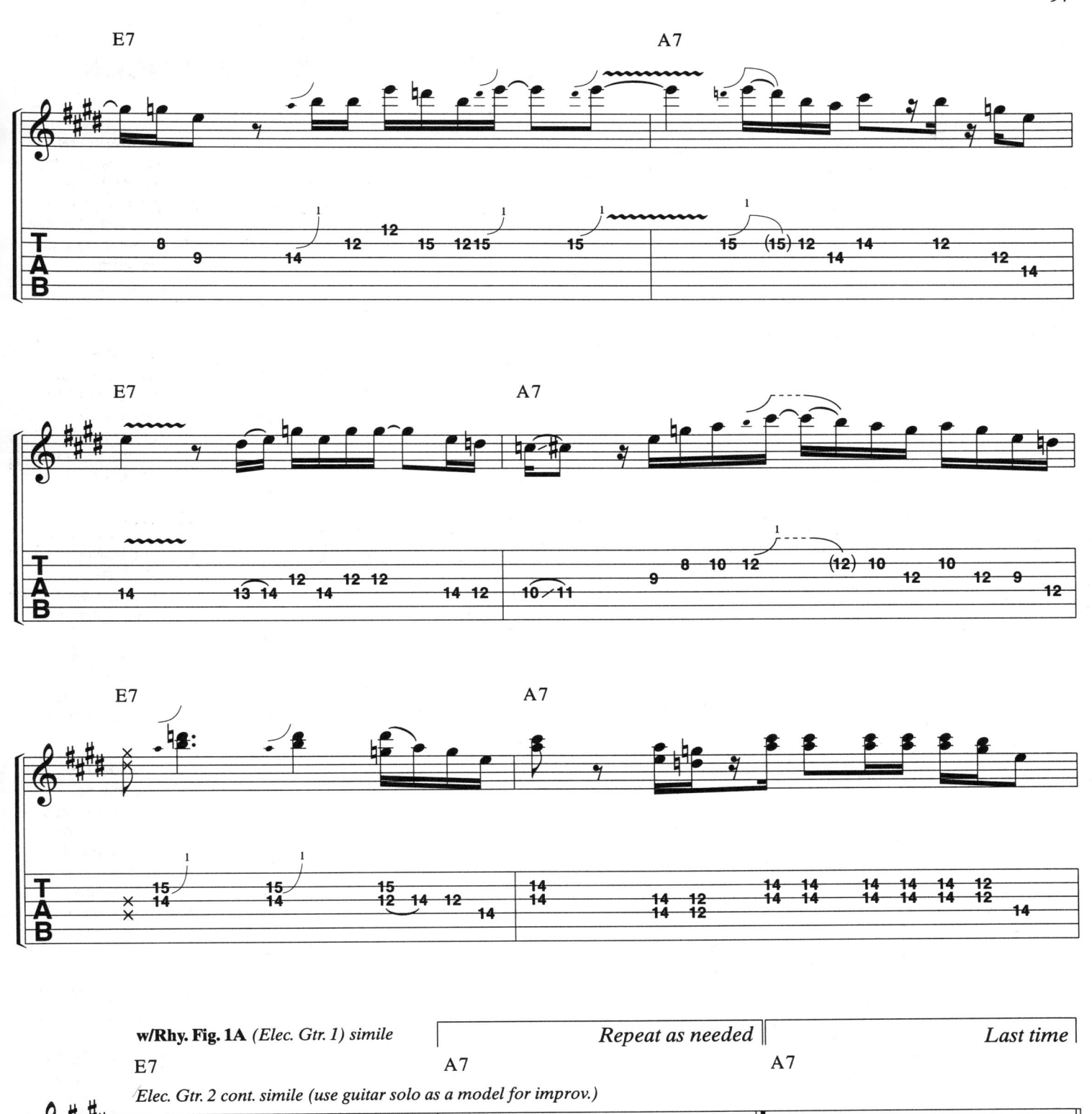

w/Rhy. Fig. 1A *(Elec. Gtr. 1) simile* — Repeat as needed — Last time

Elec. Gtr. 2 cont. simile (use guitar solo as a model for improv.)

Verse 3:
w/Rhy. Figs. 1 *(Elec. Gtr. 2)* **& 1A** *(Elec. Gtr. 1) both 2 times*

Got-ta find a wom-an be good to me, won't hide my liq-uor, try to serve me tea.

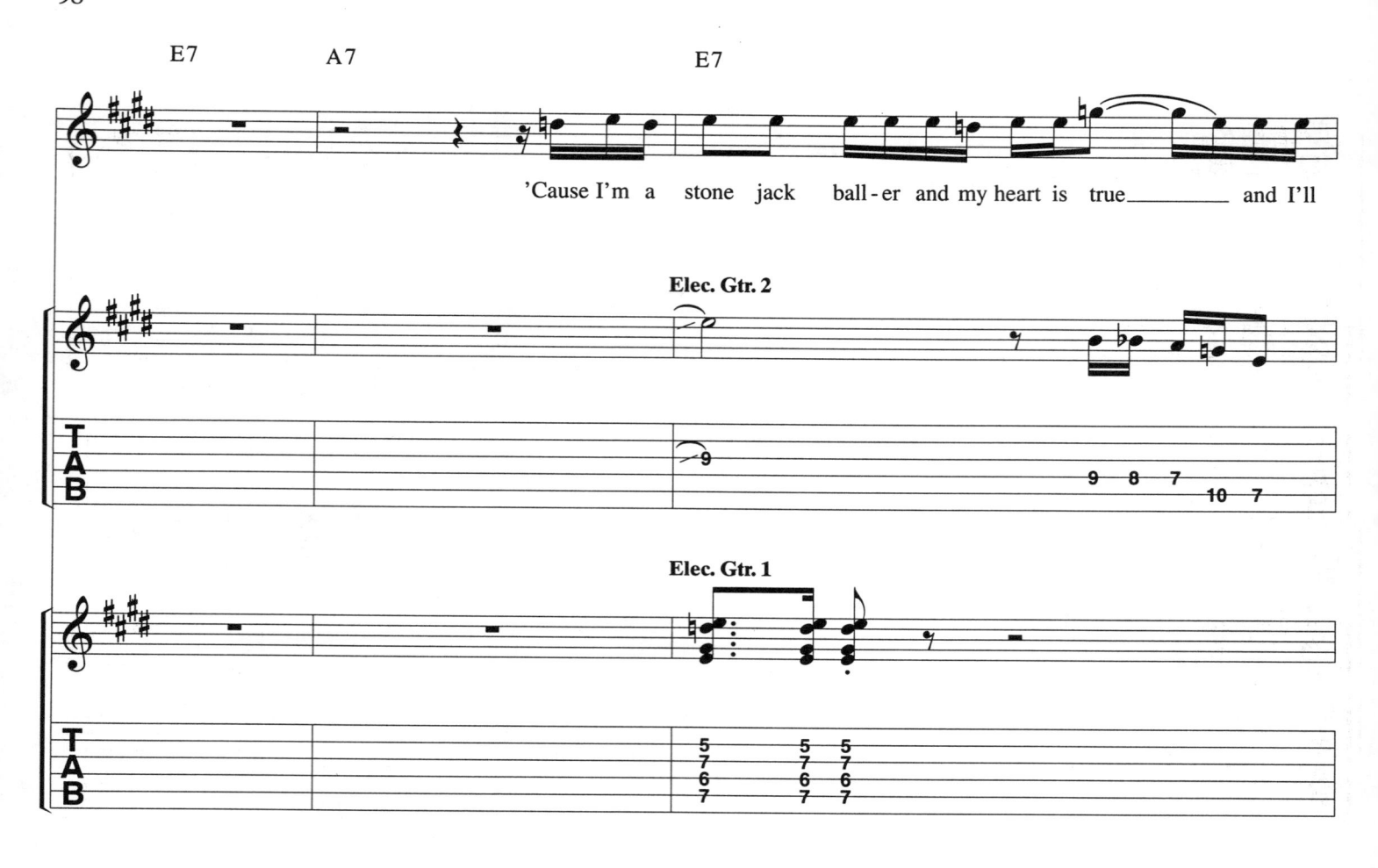

'Cause I'm a stone jack ball-er and my heart is true_____ and I'll give_ ev-'ry-thing_ that I got to you,___ yes, I will._

Easy Wind - 11 - 8

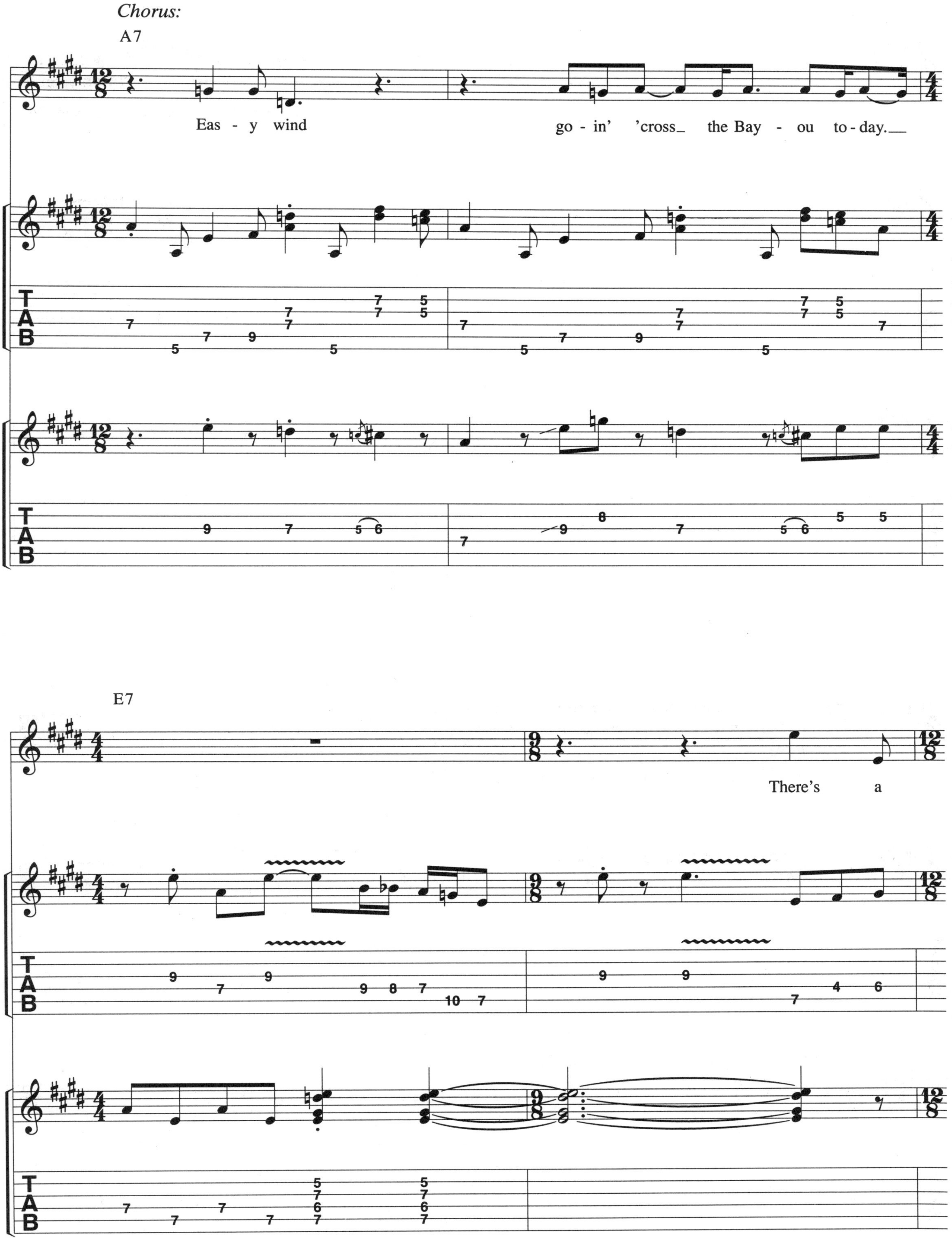
Chorus:
A7
Eas - y wind
go - in' 'cross_ the Bay - ou to - day.__
E7
There's a

whole lot-ta wom-en___ out on the streets in red___ to-day.___ And the

Easy Wind - 11 - 10

riv - er keep a - talk - in', _____ but you nev - er heard a word _ it said. _

CASEY JONES

Words by ROBERT HUNTER
Music by JERRY GARCIA

Chords: C, F, D, G, E7, Am, B♭, A7, D7, G7

Moderately ♩ = 92

Intro:

Chorus:

Driv-ing that train high on co-caine. Cas-ey Jones, you'd bet-ter watch your speed.

© 1970 (Renewed) ICE NINE PUBLISHING CO., INC.
All Rights Reserved

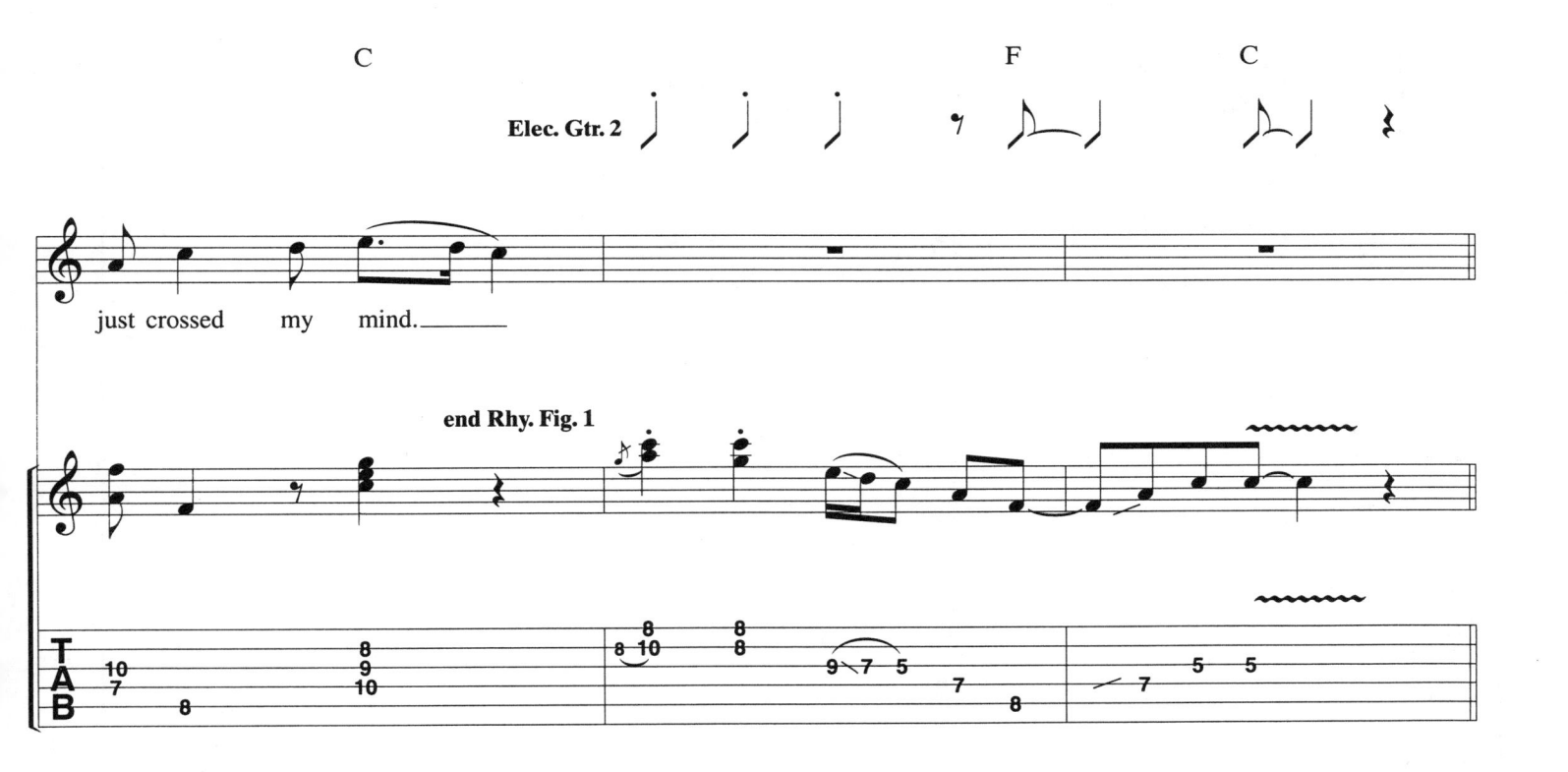

Trou-ble a-head,_ trou-ble be-hind._ And you know that no-tion just crossed my mind._

Casey Jones - 10 - 2

%% *Verse:*

*Sub. w/Rhy. Fill 1 *(Elec. Gtrs. 1, 2, & 3) Verse 2 only*

C　　　　　　　　　　　　D　　　　　　　　　　　　F

*Elec. Gtr. 2 Resume rhy. fig. simile

1. This old___ en - gine　　makes it on time,___　leaves Cen - tral Sta - tion 'bout a
2. Trou - ble a - head,_ the　　la - dy in red.___　Take my ad - vice___ you'd be
3. *See additional lyrics*

*Elec. Gtr. 1

*Elec. Gtr. 3

*Verses 1 & 3 only.

C　　　　　　　　C#　　　　　　　D

Rhy. Fill 1
Elec. Gtr. 2

Elec. Gtr. 1

Elec. Gtr. 3

Casey Jones - 10 - 3

Casey Jones - 10 - 4

F
C
high on co - caine.
Cas - ey Jones, you'd bet - ter
watch your
speed.
F
Trou - ble a - head,
trou - ble be - hind.
And you know that no - tion
hold
hold
hold
To Coda
1.
C
F
C
just crossed my mind.
Elec. Gtrs. 1 & 3
Rhy. Fig. 2
Elec. Gtr. 2
Rhy. Fig. 2A

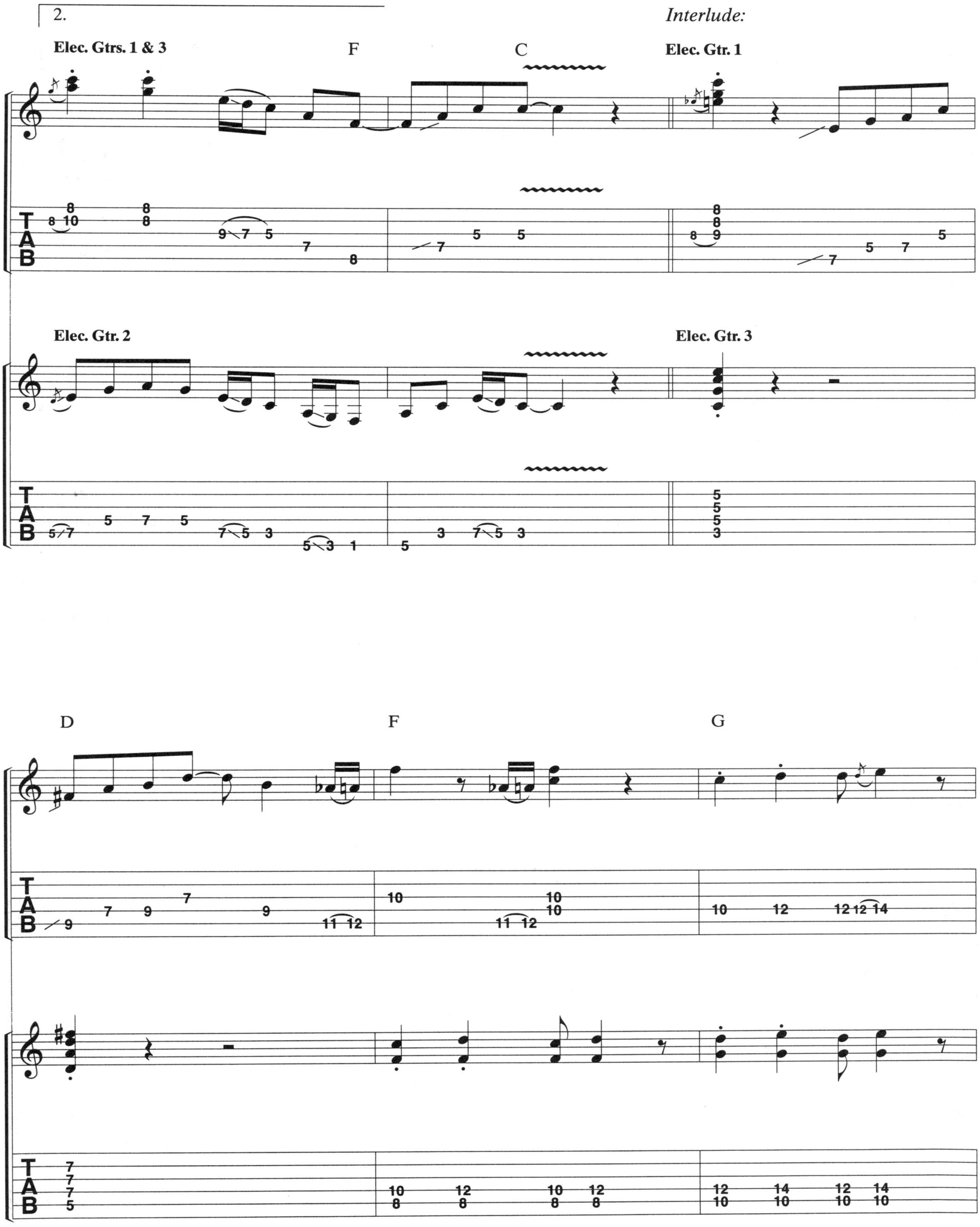
2.
Interlude:
Elec. Gtrs. 1 & 3
F
C
Elec. Gtr. 1
Elec. Gtr. 2
Elec. Gtr. 3
D
F
G

C
D
F
E7
Guitar Solo:
w/Rhy. Fig. 1 (Elec. Gtrs. 1 & 3)
Am
G
C
F
Elec. Gtr. 4
mf
"Drive your train."
C

Driving that train, high on cocaine.
Casey Jones, you'd better watch your speed. Trouble ahead, trouble behind. And you know that notion just crossed my mind.

Casey Jones - 10 - 8

110

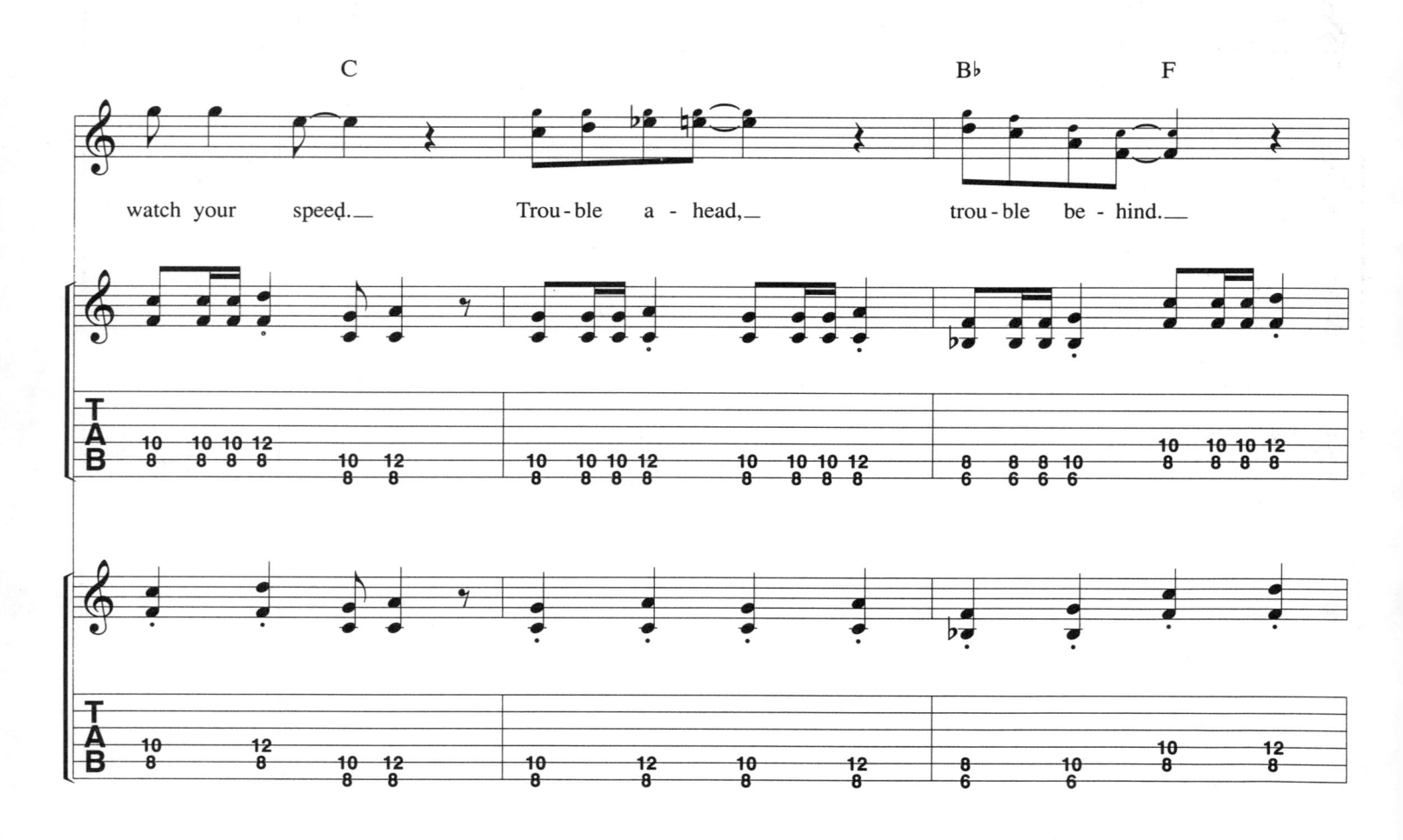

Outro:

Driv-ing that train high on co-caine. Cas-ey Jones, you'd bet-ter watch your speed. Trou-ble a-head, trou-ble be-hind.

Casey Jones - 10 - 9

Verse 3:
The trouble with you is the trouble with me.
You got two good eyes but still don't see.
Come 'round the bend you know it's the end.
The fireman screams and the engine just gleams.
(To Chorus:)

GUITAR TAB GLOSSARY **

TABLATURE EXPLANATION

READING TABLATURE: Tablature illustrates the six strings of the guitar. Notes and chords are indicated by the placement of fret numbers on a given string(s).

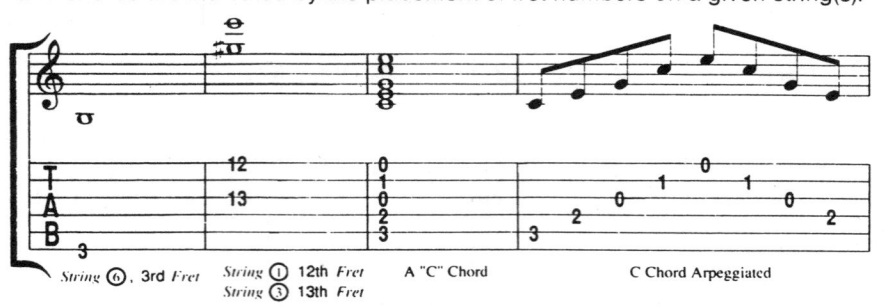

String ⑥, 3rd Fret
String ① 12th Fret
String ③ 13th Fret
A "C" Chord
C Chord Arpeggiated

BENDING NOTES

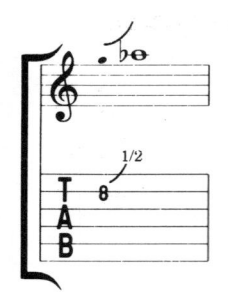

HALF STEP: Play the note and bend string one half step.*

WHOLE STEP: Play the note and bend string one whole step.

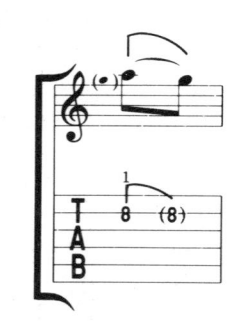

PREBEND AND RELEASE: Bend the string, play it, then release to the original note.

RHYTHM SLASHES

STRUM INDICATIONS: Strum with indicated rhythm. The chord voicings are found on the first page of the transcription underneath the song title.

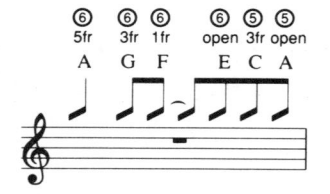

INDICATING SINGLE NOTES USING RHYTHM SLASHES: Very often single notes are incorporated into a rhythm part. The note name is indicated above the rhythm slash with a fret number and a string indication.

*A half step is the smallest interval in Western music; it is equal to one fret. A whole step equals two frets.

**By Kenn Chipkin and Aaron Stang

ARTICULATIONS

HAMMER ON: Play lower note, then "hammer on" to higher note with another finger. Only the first note is attacked.

PULL OFF: Play higher note, then "pull off" to lower note with another finger. Only the first note is attacked.

LEGATO SLIDE: Play note and slide to the following note. (Only first note is attacked).

PALM MUTE: The note or notes are muted by the palm of the pick hand by lightly touching the string(s) near the bridge.

ACCENT: Notes or chords are to be played with added emphasis.

DOWN STROKES AND UPSTROKES: Notes or chords are to be played with either a downstroke (⊓) or upstroke (∨) of the pick.

© 1990 Beam Me Up Music
c/o CPP/Belwin, Inc. Miami, Florida 33014
International Copyright Secured   Made in U.S.A.   All Rights Reserved